'In the wake of the hysteria of school jihadi t
this timely and well-researched book "lifts the
"bad Muslim mothers", with powerful storie:
commitment against the c

**Heidi Safia Mirza, Professor of Race, Faith and Culture,
Goldsmiths, University of London**

'This groundbreaking book gives us a rare and compelling insight into
the views of Muslim mothers about their children's education at a time
when there is a paucity of research in this area. *Muslim Mother's and their
Children's Schooling* is an essential read for all professionals who work
in education and wish to understand better the needs of the increasingly
diverse pupil population they serve.'

Sameena Choudry, Founder of Equitable Education

'Suma Din has penned an exceptional book that rightfully explores
an important area of research and policy thinking. The findings of her
study are of great importance, not just to policymakers but also Muslim
communities in general. The voices of Muslim women in relation to their
children's schooling are told in an articulate and insightful manner, all in a
process to help improve understanding, trust and engagement. This book is
highly recommended for teachers, parents, policymakers and researchers,
all working away to understand the myriad issues facing mothers, children
and the education system.'

**Professor Tahir Abbas, Senior Research Fellow at the
Royal United Services Institute, London**

Muslim Mothers and their Children's Schooling

Muslim Mothers and their Children's Schooling
Suma Din

 is an imprint of

First published in 2017 by the UCL Institute of Education Press, University College London, 20 Bedford Way, London WC1H 0AL

www.ucl-ioe-press.com

British Library Cataloguing in Publication Data:
A catalogue record for this publication is available from the British Library

ISBNs
978-1-85856-795-2 (paperback)
978-1-85856-796-9 (PDF eBook)
978-1-85856-797-6 (ePub eBook)
978-1-85856-798-3 (Kindle eBook)

Typeset by Quadrant Infotech (India) Pvt Ltd
Printed by CPI Group (UK) Ltd, Croydon, CR0 4YY
Cover design by EMC Design. Image courtesy of eFesenko / Alamy Stock Photo.

Contents

Acknowledgements

The nature of producing a book like this involves the help and support of several people; some who influenced the contents over a decade ago, others involved directly and recently. I am thankful to all those teachers, school governors, headteachers, parents, students and friends I have had thought-provoking conversations with, for being part of the journey that has culminated in this title.

Long before the contents can take shape, someone has to believe in the seed of an idea, in order for it to be planted and take root. For that initial belief, I thank two eminent scholars, Professors Carol Vincent and Tahir Abbas. Without their questions and advice at the gestation stage, this seed may well have been put aside. In a similar vein, my thanks extends to several researchers, writers, teachers and activists for mother-centred discussions, and in particular I owe much to Saleema Burney, Anisa Ather and Khadija Afzal, who read and commented on parts of the earliest drafts.

On a practical level, I am hugely indebted to the gatekeepers, NR, MR, IM, RH and SA, who trusted in the project and opened doors for me to interview mothers they knew. They made time alongside their jobs and commitments for all the correspondence required to secure interviews and focus group participants. From providing interview spaces, to watching over participants' toddlers, their help was instrumental during the research phase.

My heartfelt thanks go to the 51 mothers – trusting, enthusiastic and committed – they overcame several obstacles to come to participate. Thank you for giving without measure. I'm equally grateful to the two earnest mothers, managers of the 'Muslim Mamas' Facebook groups, for their contribution. Together, all 53 mothers brought the idea to life.

Sincere appreciation goes to the editor, Gillian Klein for her editorial work to make this book what it is. I have had the good fortune to learn from her wisdom and experience in the process.

I am grateful to close friends who never showed any weariness of the subject and whose assurances at difficult times made the pages turn, one by one. Finally, I am grateful to my extended family for accommodating the unsociable occupation of writing, with optimism and faith in the subject. Writing about mothers would not be complete without acknowledging my own mother's support over the years, and her patience with the unconventional times I've kept recently. Likewise, my children have participated in the subject of this book, unwittingly since their nursery years through to their university education, and our conversations are inseparable from this work. I end with thanking Asad for his assistance at every level, unconditional and constant, as always.

About the author

Suma Din is an author, freelance researcher and educator. She worked with parents for a decade in the Adult Learning sector delivering Family Learning, English courses and CPD training. Her work with Muslim women and girls spans over 20 years in community-focused education programmes.

As a non-fiction author, her titles for children and teaching resources support a variety of subjects including RE, global citizenship and history. For adults, she writes on motherhood, women and spirituality. Suma has consulted on both UK and overseas educational publishing projects.

Preface

In this book I set out to present contemporary narratives that relate the lived reality of Muslim mothers to a readership involved in the education and welfare of their children. To communicate, where a void exists. For those genuinely interested in hearing marginal voices, those who recognize the impact family has on students' wellbeing, the personal narratives I present are the frame on which all else is hung.

I approach the subject from an unconventional place: as a practitioner in Adult Education, an English teacher, writer, member of a faith community and, of course a mother – competing roles depending on place and time. As hard as one might try to draw boundaries between professional and private lives, reading candid passages in the works of educational scholars confirms a truth – not universally acknowledged – that the personal and professional, public and private, are never really separate. So this Preface makes no attempt at aloof professionalism or objectivity, but tries rather to communicate the raison d'etre of this book.

My impetus to write the book has evolved gradually over the past decade as I moved among my many roles. While delivering Family Learning programmes I encountered mothers from many minority backgrounds, heard and observed aspects of their mothering and their children's schooling. In certain parts of areas of deprivation, the mothers were predominantly Muslims from the Asian subcontinent. Our frequent interactions sustained and increased my interest in their relationship with their children's schools. Beneath my professional identity lies two decades of working both voluntarily and freelance on projects with Muslim mothers and teenage girls. Be it for faith-related programmes or parenting workshops, such experiences meant sharing their challenges and dilemmas on a regular basis. Peel that layer away and my personal world as a mother, with three children educated in the state sector, has entailed countless conversations and opportunities to be involved with schools as a parent and parent-governor. I revisit these starting points in relevant parts of the book and present them here as a context to my multifaceted and subjective research.

My Masters study – *Social Justice and Education* – motivated me further. I returned to university 20 years after I gained my postgraduate teaching qualification and had the opportunity to explore the literature and concepts of this discipline. Combined with my grass-roots, professional experiences of a decade earlier, this area of study gave me the idea of researching mothers. Public discourse about Muslim women – and by extension mothers – and inaccurate articles and documentaries that speak in absolutes, pressed me on. As a Muslim mother myself, there were many questions I wanted answers to. Surely there is space between the ivory tower and the gritty work as a practitioner to accommodate one's *own* reality as a point of reference?

This book opens a window on the thoughts, struggles, contributions and lives of mothers who are absent from public discourse. I hope its insights facilitate a nuanced understanding of home–school relations. I hope also that it will give researchers, policymakers and those working with Muslim families a path into new territory. And that once there, the blurred view of Muslim mothers will come into focus. A perspective on the subject is the best outcome I could hope for from a book like this, which does not set out to prove or disprove a particular theory.

It is true that there is a growing body of research *about* Muslim women, but we seldom hear *from* them. The need to improve communication and understanding between Muslim parents and those teaching their children, is the guiding principle of my research. Communication has multiple meanings, depending on the structures within which it takes place. Recognized channels exist to encourage a free flow of relevant 'news' in schools: electronic, paper, phone, websites and the yearly set appointments. Yet some types of communication still exist only at the margin, in an unnamed, grey silhouetted area not signposted in the school prospectus, nor accounted for in an Ofsted category, an area that is difficult to define or capture in one image. What do we call the space where teachers ask parents questions 'off the record' at the threshold to their classroom at the end of a day? What do we call the space where parents who don't want to go through official channels to express their concerns, stop you on your way into your car, at a school fete, in a supermarket, to tell all? How do we define these spaces and modes of communication? Such questions have motivated and at the same time troubled me and made me wonder why these spaces exist in the first place? From my own experience I would argue that they grow when there are too many barriers – real or perceived – between the school and the parents.

This space also comes about because of fears and assumptions, which often turn out to be unfounded. Thoughts and issues not readily discussed publicly are nonetheless important – in some cases especially. When a teacher wants to sound someone out about whether a particular attitude is faith related or culture related, there is no manual or policy document to help them, and these off-the-record spaces become sites of learning and bringing people together on a long-term basis. At its best it is a site of inclusion, dialogue and mutual respect – these are values one hopes it will engender. In reality, school is often a site of mobility, where some stereotypes are reinforced and lines of segregation creep in from outside.

I conclude this Preface with an illustration of the personal/public binary. The following vignette captures my experience delivering an inset in a London primary school. The inset was on using RE resources from Key Stage 1 and 2 to teach Islam.

Lost in turnips?

Two hours into the staff inset and the presentation was coming to an end. The condensed, tightly packaged account of the main beliefs, festivals and ideas for contextualizing the Qur'an and Ramadan had been delivered through the PowerPoint, resources and intermittent dialogue. As one does at the end of a session, I asked:

'Any other questions, we still have a bit of time?'

It was a full catch: with several questions on anticipated themes – protocols about using the Qur'an in class, the two Eids, prayer rituals, and so on, but one question stood out. A teacher who hadn't spoken before raised her hand from the furthest point of the semi-circle, cleared her throat and proceeded:

'I take a YR2 class and we were doing some food tasting. I'd sent letters home to say what we were doing … but there was this one kid who said he was told not to touch anything – and he didn't, I mean he wouldn't. So, I wanted to ask …' she shuffled forward on her chair, lowered her head, as one does before delivering bad news, and asked: 'Can Muslim children … like can they touch vegetables? I mean is it alright, or aren't they supposed to?'

I repeated her question for those sitting at the other end of the semi-circle – and to make sure I had heard it correctly. Amongst the answers and observations racing through my mind, I began my answer, suspecting that this was another case of 'lost in translation' on the part of the child. It was 'lost' on the teacher too.

'Yes', I replied, 'Muslim children can touch vegetables, and pulses, and grains, and just about every edible thing on earth if the need arises.'

But I had to say more.

'Growing up with two other languages as well as English, this seems to me like a case of a young child mistranslating something their parent has said. Maybe mum or dad made an arbitrary comment, in Arabic, let's say, not to touch anyone's food at school, or not to eat just anything someone gives you at school, which filtered through a 6-year-old's head into a rather odd sounding: "I'm not allowed to touch any food".'

In my head I heard some of the daily phrases my mother uses and the absurdity of trying to translate them. I continued:

'I know, when I think of phrases from Bengali and Urdu, if I translate them literally, they'll sound odd – translation's complex at the best of times. But I can assure you, there has never been a problem of touching vegetables in the Muslim past, nor is there in the present nor will there be in the future.'

She smiled and nodded her understanding. But something inside me shifted, from optimism to reality: is this where we've arrived? How did we get to a stage where a child's faith identity is so alien that the most normal of norms invites a question like this?

That morning reminded me of a friend's story about being invited to visit a primary school class as a 'guest' from a different faith group. As she made her way down the corridor, looking for the classroom, she heard a teacher's voice from a doorway: 'The Muslim's arrived, the Muslim's arrived, children.' One will never know what preparation went on beforehand, but the children asked revealing questions, as the guest sat on the hot seat to answer: '*Do Muslims wear shoes? Do Muslims have sofas? Do Muslims eat chips? Do Muslims brush their teeth?*' The last one proved the most interesting: the guest, as well as being 'the Muslim' was also a dentist. Wryly she lifted her coat and showed them her trainers: 'Erm, do these count as shoes?' she joked with the children. Where would these questions sit in the debate about 'nature' or 'nurture'? Do children have an inbuilt ability to 'other' or is it coming from somewhere else?

And thus my premise for this book: to reduce the gap, to shift – if that's possible – educators' perceptions, which if left can cause alienation and otherness to grow. Misinformation is one thing. But as time has gone on, the otherness has become a void filled with whatever is in the air at that particular time.

I have sought to bring into the educational sphere the diverging and reinforcing voices of 53 mothers from various ethnic and socio-economic backgrounds – some professional, some not, some educated, some with limited literacy. My aim is to offer an insight into their positions. I hoped to facilitate research and practice about Muslim children and their families. Inevitably these voices, like any voices from a group, can only be 'samples'. Nowhere do I claim that they are representative of all mothers, or all Muslim women, or even their ethnic group. If there is one unifying factor in the group of participants who willingly gave me their time, it is this: they all care about their children's education and all cared enough about the schools they attend to talk to me for the purpose of improving communication.

Introduction

I'm a Muslim and a mum ... and there's a responsibility of not just raising children but raising them in a certain way, so we have a lot more expectations on ourselves for this life and the next.

(Nilofer)

Personal voices for public spaces; mothers talking about education and school. In essence, this is what this book is about. The content is based on empirical research, which is prioritized above theoretical debates. I present 53 mothers' narratives here to share hitherto unheard experiences and thus create a vocal bridge between them and the school world.

I have used their narratives as a platform to extrapolate themes because I want to present their authentic voice. In *Writing the Motherline* (2006), the relationship between mothers and their daughters' educational trajectories relies primarily on the former's accounts. O'Brien and Sawandar explain why they chose to do their study this way:

> ... to be human is to be interpretive. Searching meanings from inside out captures the hermeneutic or interpretive understanding of people's life experiences, viewing reality through the lens of the participants and generating ideas and information through their own voices. Thus the linkages of objectivity and lived experience, intersubjective construction of meaning, and identity formation are articulated and illuminated.

(2006: 15)

In the voices heard throughout the chapters, the internal perspective of the women I interviewed is prioritized over popular debates about what constitutes a family, or about the socially constructed institution of motherhood (Abbey and O'Reilly, 1998; Ruddick, 1989; Lazzare, 1976). For readers who want to explore such angles, there are three decades worth of scholarship. By contrast, motherhood as an experience – as an act of 'becoming' – has, according to motherhood scholars, been marginalized in research. Yet there *is* a steady flow of research into their lives. Hollway (2015), for example, constructs motherhood as 'an ontology centred around becoming' to understand what happened for the 19 women in her study who become mothers.

In Chapter 1 I discuss the centrality of parents and the family in a child's educational development – in the widest sense. I also position mothers in research. I explore the policy contexts relevant to the study of mothers for whom gender, faith, ethnicity and socio-economic status are potential sites of distancing and othering in the public domain. The concept of intersectionality thus enters the discussion as I look at multiple sites of marginalization and 'argue for an understanding of how intersectional forces and discourses shape individual and collective experiences of motherhood' (Veazey, 2015: 8). Veazey concludes that 'motherhood is therefore a rich case study for looking at the way social locations intersect, interact and change'.

My rationale for exploring the experience of a group of mothers according to their faith rests upon two facts: first, their children constitute the largest minority faith presence in UK schools – ONS census figures show that 8.1 per cent of all school-aged children in England and Wales are Muslim (Sundas, 2015) – and if we are to understand their backgrounds, we need to engage with and understand those who are central to their lives. Second, this group receives a disproportionate amount of negative press. An anomaly exists: a void of self-representation amidst a vortex of troubling articles and media. In Chapter 2 I wrestle with such issues and present the scriptural evidence, to establish how motherhood is understood from a Muslim faith perspective.

Theoretically it is 'parents' who are in partnership with their children's school. In this book, I look into the partnership between mothers and school, choosing to highlight mothers and not fathers because research has consistently shown that 'parenting' refers overwhelmingly to the work of mothers across ethnicities and class. This is not to diminish the important contribution fathers – who have a deep sense of responsibility to their children – make, but globally the mother is the primary caregiver in a child's upbringing. This is the most important reason for focusing on mothers, although there are more.

I raise the matter of positionality again in Chapter 3, in which I introduce the 53 mothers of approximately 160 children. The chapter also details their educational levels, professional status, involvement in voluntary work and the 'work' of raising a family. In today's society it is ironic that doing such work equates to doing nothing – to 'being lazy' and 'economically inactive' – but any perceived negligence or failure in such 'work' brings heavy scrutiny and sanctions from every sector of public services. Although the mothers in my study are grouped together by their faith, their identities are, on the one hand, specific but on the other hand they are what makes the collective, collective. Gilroy captures this anomaly succinctly: 'Above all, identity can help us to comprehend the formation of that fateful pronoun "we" and to reckon with the patterns of inclusion and exclusion that it cannot but help to create' (Gilroy, 1997: 302). Chapter 3 contextualizes the mothers' voices within their ethnicity, demographics and educational status.

Chapters 4–7 are assembled around the themes that arose from my interviews with the mothers. It was there that they exercised their agency, interpreting my questions as they wished, taking discussions along lines that meant something to them and using – as they did in the focus groups – peer dynamics to probe and challenge each other. Accordingly, Chapter 4 begins with their take on their own identity in relation to how they feel they are viewed. It also considers their understanding of what education means to them. This underpins their expectations of the education system and together the two strands inform what they prioritize when making school choices for their children. On the micro level, Chapter 5 presents the mothers' experiences of their general communication and relationships with the school: surveillance, playground politics and a reflexive exploration of involvement with the school community. Chapter 6 details their interactions regarding academic matters and focuses on specific curriculum areas that present a challenge because of a difference in certain principles and values. Sex and Relationships Education (SRE), parents' evening and behaviour-related communication were the aspects most commonly spoken about. These form the themes I discuss in Chapter 6. In closing, Chapter 7 broadens out the discussion to address themes that arose in several narratives that I had not been expecting. These relate to children's wider educational context.

The breadth of subject matter covered here is shaped entirely by the participants' responses during our interviews and the focus group discussions. The chapters are constructed according to their choice of anecdotes. So the book seeks to capture who these 53 women are in the context of educating their children.

Chapter 1

In sight and in mind

Finding the mother

I want them to see me as a parent who is bothered.

(Tahira)

People always ask the children if they are ok, but no one asks the mum.

(Naila)

If you're bothered, the teacher's bothered. If you're not, they're not.

(Dina)

Education is not just maths and English, but helping fellow humans, helping yourself and nurturing your spiritual side as well.

(Hodan)

Families, however they are defined, are the bedrock of society. Children come from families – they never have, nor will they be sole entities, however individualistic society becomes. They are part of a network of caregivers who make decisions for them, nurture, teach and protect them. Whether the bond is biological or legal, the fact remains that the 'family' constructed around a child plays a significant role in their development.

In terms of raising a child, the 'family' can comprise numerous realities: children can be raised, among others, by grandfathers, adoptive parents, single mothers or fathers or, most commonly, a mother and a father. In this book I look at one particular caregiver: the mother. This is not to diminish the importance of other carers who successfully raise children. Instead, I focus on mothers because of the universal connection between them and children, a connection that transcends time, culture and place. The importance of the mother in terms of her child's wellbeing is overlooked in public discourse about children's education.

I begin this chapter by considering the position of parents – as opposed to mothers – to establish how they are situated in relation to their children's education. Three ways in particular are prioritized. First, I briefly analyse the legal duty upon schools to ensure that they adopt a general ethos of inclusivity and do not discriminate against pupils with protected characteristics. Then I explore the parent–school relationship of rights and responsibilities and how this connection has been researched by scholars. Using these perspectives I show why parental involvement is highly relevant to educators and those influencing policy in a number of ways. Finally, I consider why mothers are important as a group and how they form their identities. I analyse the latter by using an intersectional framework that accommodates multiple aspects – namely, race, gender and class – which converge, or intersect, in the process of identity formation. I continue to use the framework throughout the book as a theoretical tool to understand the narratives of the mothers I interviewed.

The Equality Act 2010/Public Sector Equality Duty 2011

The Equality Act 2010 – and by extension the Public Sector Equality Duty – have made it incumbent upon educators to make schools inclusive institutions, and to ensure that students with protected characteristics are not discriminated against. The protected characteristics relate to both a school's students and employees. They are: gender, sex, race, disability, sexual orientation, gender reassignment, religion or belief, pregnancy or maternity. The Act also quantifies four types of unlawful behaviour: 'direct discrimination, indirect discrimination, harassment and victimisation' (Equality Act, 2010).

The duty on schools to publish their own equalities priorities once a year, in line with what is relevant to their size and culture, allows on the one hand for less bureaucracy – previously three separate policies were required on disability, race and gender – and opens up on the other a debate about subjectivity and how decisions are made. As it stands, however, the legal imperative for pupils with protected characteristics to be protected is directly relevant to looking at parents of pupils who may have several such characteristics. The Equality Act aims to 'eliminate discrimination' and 'advance equality of opportunity between people who share a protected characteristic and people who do not'. Most notably it seeks to 'foster good relations across all characteristics' (Equality Act, 2010). These laws that govern the treatment of pupils in schools do just that: they deal with pupils. Yet daily life blurs the distinctions between a pupil and the family they come from. So, while parents are not explicitly mentioned, their influence on and relationships with their children should be significant to the discourse on schools' equalities duties. With the diversity in schools in urban areas increasing year on year, it becomes necessary to recognize the position of parents in relation to the Act itself.

Laws and legislation are bound to the time and place they are made in, but the need to include parents – and mothers in particular – exists beyond the parameters of space and time. For the educative process to be holistic and nurture the whole child, the home setting – where 75 per cent of the child's waking time is spent (Pre-school Learning Alliance, 2007) – needs to be understood. There has been a shift away, however, from acknowledging and exploring this need, particularly when the position of a family intersects concerns about social justice. Examining changes in teacher training, Bagley and Beach (2015) argue that priorities in teacher education have changed over the past 30 years, reflecting the neo-liberal priorities of reaching targets, the marketization of education and managerialism (Ball, 2008), all of which are geared towards making schools compete. Their analysis suggests that:

> In a rapidly changing and complex multi-cultural society, England's teachers are now only being equipped with a predominantly horizontal knowledge discourse and are thus less prepared for defining, assessing and, if necessary, responsibly adjusting their teaching to improve learning for marginalised and disadvantaged students and addressing questions of social justice.
>
> (Bagley and Beach, 2015: 12)

And it is precisely from 'questions of social justice' that research about parents and their relationship with schools arises. The developments, if taken as the authors present, seem regressive in terms of improving awareness about parents who sit at the axis of disadvantage.

This shift away from theorizing social justice issues morphs into another area of school life: inspection criteria. In contrast to the general ethos of the Equality Act, extensive research has found that examination by Ofsted has moved away from prioritizing inclusion and diversity. Chris Wilkins' analysis suggests that Ofsted is evading the issue of race/racism and lowering its status in the statutory guidance. The result is that less attention is being paid to it. Wilkins asserts:

> The distribution of positive and negative references in Ofsted reports to equality/diversity provision provides a strong indication that Ofsted's claim that it treats equality and diversity as being 'at the heart of everything it does' (Ofsted 2009) is unfounded. The evidence from this review of 200+ reports carried out over a period of five years (encompassing two different inspection frameworks) is that it is at best treated as a peripheral matter that

has little or no impact on overall inspection outcomes. The data provided here suggests that the possibility for another dynamic operating in inspectors' consideration.

(Wilkins, 2014: 258)

Taken together, these two examples highlight a divergence: while policies might prioritize notions of inclusivity, practical measures in teacher training and the way a school's 'success' is measured are moving away from making inclusion a priority. Legal requirements are therefore limited in their scope of affecting attitudes. And without a change in attitudes, sinkholes in inclusion and cohesion can and will appear with disturbing ease. No amount of policies, checks or measures can truly capture intangible 'othering' – yet it is still legislation we must look to, if only for terms of reference.

The home–school agreement and the Schools Standards Framework Act

According to sections 110 and 111 of the Schools Standards and Framework Act 1988, it is a duty upon schools, including grant-maintained schools and academies, to publish a contract that parents of registered children must sign: the home–school agreement. Statutory guidance from the Department for Education offers the following guidelines regarding the subject matter the contract should mention:

- the school's aims and values
- the school's responsibilities towards its pupils who are of compulsory school age
- the responsibility of each pupil's parents
- what the school expects of its pupils.

It is part of the governing body's role to ensure that the school publishes and parents sign this agreement. Although the language differs from school to school, contracts are broadly based on these guidelines, which state that the school's responsibilities are to educate and see to the welfare of children, while parents are expected to support their child's education.

A review of home–school agreement contracts shows that there is an assumption that parents will have the talents and experiences to match the needs of the curriculum, the language it is delivered in and the ethos of the school. Furthermore, the expectation that parents will be involved in their child's education to this extent is in itself problematic.

A generation back, neither government policy nor popular culture had placed the responsibility of education on parents' shoulders as explicitly as it did after the 1988 Education Act, which advocated greater powers to parents in tandem with increasing the marketization of education. From the Conservative party's neoliberal policies (Ball 2008), to New Labour's edicts on education, several policy documents built the case for parents to become consumers, to exercise their choice and to take responsibility for their children's education (Vincent, 1996; Crozier, 1999). Many critical papers detail the social inequalities of the increasing marketization of schools (Ball, 2003), of increased choice and competition, which position the parent as 'consumer' (Gewirtz *et al.*, 1994; Edwards and Gillies, 2011).

The parent's role as consumer is built on an economic premise. It defines education as a mechanism to produce workers capable of competing in the global labour market. While there is vocal opposition to the marketization of education, those who support the free market have traditionally supported greater parental participation and accountability – for those parents who possess the social capital or knowledge of the way the education system works and who can thus manoeuvre successfully within it.

An alternative perspective on the role of parents, however, sees them as primarily responsible for their children's education. According to section 7 of the Education Act 1991, the law places a duty on parents to educate their children, either by sending them to full-time school from the age of 5 or by providing education themselves by alternative means. The home–school agreement serves to formalize parents' responsibility in the shape of a tangible agreement, particularly for those who might neither be aware or concerned that their child's education is their responsibility. Quite a shift in perspective. From this angle, it could justifiably be argued that schools are in fact helping parents, rather than the other way round (David, 1999). Halsey and Young (1997) make a case for the moral and ethical importance of the family to a child's wellbeing. Their view – that the family is at the 'heart of the moral economy' (1997: 785) – supports the view that the primary responsibility for a child's welfare, which includes education, sits squarely with the parents.

The move to increased parental involvement in schools has come about through successive government policies. It started with the 1967 Plowden Report, which popularized the view of parents as a 'source of potential educational benefit' (in Ouston and Hood, 2000). Education Acts during the 1980s, culminating in the Education Reform Act 1988, made it mandatory for schools to give parents information about their child's attainment in the National Curriculum. They also increased parents' powers as governors and voting rights regarding the school's status about remaining in the Local Education Authority. The rationale given by both the Conservative and New Labour Governments was to improve standards in education. White Papers such as *Choice and Diversity in Schools* (1992), for example, state that the changes for greater choice and diversity will 'inevitably raise standards'. That the 'importance and rights of parents are fully recognised' is a thread that runs through the document and into later publications. It eventually became firmly rooted in parents' psyches, as the mushrooming of media articles about 'parent power' evidenced. Whether the message of choice and rights reached all parents is doubtful, however. As research on the home–school agreement has shown, marginalized or working-class parents rarely engage with the choices because they prioritize other factors such as: close proximity to the school, their own work patterns or responsibility for other children. Some simply do not know their rights (Gerwitz *et al.*, 1995).

Whether a right or a responsibility, parental involvement is seen as having a beneficial effect on children's attainment and progress (Goodall and Vorhaus, 2011). In *The Review of Best Practice in Parental Engagement*, the authors suggest ways for schools to 'engage' parents as opposed to inviting them in for set appointments. This participatory model is shared by advocates who hold parents responsible for their children's education and look not only to schools for better achievement. As Goodall (2015b) points out, 75 per cent of a child's time is spent outside school and what parents are doing with them can nurture their learning and development.

It is surprising, then, that Ofsted no longer requires secondary schools to 'engage' with parents if they are to be rated outstanding. It still retains this criterion for primary schools, however (Ofsted, 2015). Such changes have been criticized as removing the necessity to engage with parents and be made accountable to them (Goodall, 2015a). Furthermore, if the role of schools is to be understood in the widest sense:

> as centres of civic responsibility and as educative institutions – schools that foster and respond to the participation of parents and students with teachers and other local stakeholders, in the making of decisions about what education is for, what it means to be educated and what, and how, students should learn (Ball, 2013), then the call to strengthen community engagement, work with parents, increase cumulative learning, is justifiable.

Consistent with these findings is the government's policy document *Every Parent Matters* (DfES, 2007), which moves beyond stating the need for parents' involvement to *supporting* parents to become more involved. The document focuses on the wide-reaching, positive ways parents can influence their children, as well as offering advice and information about support services through which they can access help. The 'parent-friendly' look of the document and its tone of warm encouragement and apparent understanding of their challenges is problematic. It assumes that all parents have the ability and time to support their children in the way it advocates. This masks the deep structural inequalities that bar involvement, be they economic or about health, work and family contexts. Parental involvement requires that social injustices be tackled by policies outside a school's remit. This is a huge subject in its own right, beyond the discussion in this book.

Social justice and parental engagement

Approaching the parent–school relationship through the principles of social justice is, however, necessary. It has also revealed areas where parents lack agency, bringing their struggles and realities to the fore. Whether these struggles are because of ethnicity, class, location, gender or a combination of factors, the fact remains that there are barriers to engagement that can contribute to unequal access and outcomes for students. Concurrently, research into this field takes the school's perspective into account and questions why parents are not involved (Crozier and Davies, 2007).

Academic scholars who have taken a close look at how marginalized parents manage their relationship with schools offer some answers. In Crozier and Reay's *Activating Participation* (2005), for example, contributors shed light on a tapestry of experiences that testify to the complex ways families interact with schools and teachers. The studies explore *what* constitutes participation and *how* it is affected, drawing on how parents navigate their involvement and considering their social class and ethnicity. Several chapters in this book draw on empirical research that focuses on the experience of mothers in particular.

In investigations into the identity formation of school-aged pupils, theorists have similarly put the relationship between the home, local communities and schools under the microscope. Chanda-Gool (2006), Crozier and Davies (2007), Abbas (2007) and Bhatti (2011) all look at the way home and school relationships impact on students' education, aspirations, identity and achievement. Their findings point to such hurdles as parents' education and/ or language levels, as well as feelings of being judged or unwelcome. Over the past decade, the deficit perspective of what students and their families are *not* has been replaced by a focus on who Muslim pupils *are*, in their own words. These studies take various approaches: integration (Abbas, 2007), citizenship (Modood, 2005), sub-cultures (Shain, 2003 and 2012) and how Muslim teenage girls strategize within teacher surveillance (Mirza and Meetoo, 2013). Gender is brought to the fore by Kaye Haw (1998), who takes a feminist approach in her ethnographic study that examines equality issues for Muslim girls in British state schools as compared to Muslim girls' schools.

Chanda-Gool's (2006) approach generates more holistic data, including students and parents and those who influence them outside school. Her research on South Asian communities sets out a number of aims: to understand how South Asian pupils, parents, teachers and community workers feel about their identity and how their voices can be used to enhance understanding and education in schools. Chanda-Gool's study explores responses from members of different South Asian communities: Bangladeshi, Pakistani, Indian. It provides data on three themes: 'the reaffirming response', the 'contradictory and compromised response' and the 'dynamic response'. The children in her study, predominantly from Year 6, spoke of their pride in and loyalty to their heritage, as well as the 'fundamental problem with the separation between the home and school' (2006: 130). Parents and community spokespeople, meanwhile, articulated their desire to see greater cultural awareness in schools to help South Asian children develop their self-esteem and a healthy identity. Chanda-Gool advocates practical solutions in the classroom to tackle the 'disjuncture' (*ibid*) parents, teachers and pupils feel. While her data and discussion about the types of responses illuminate the importance of culture and religion for South Asians, there is a sense towards the end of the study that her initial aim of understanding how South Asians felt about themselves was rapidly overtaken by concerns about how schools understood and worked *with* them (2006: 134). Her assertion that 'it is vital to understand the link between identity, self-esteem, motivation and attainment' is also shared by others. In Maurice Cole's *Towards the Compassionate School* (2015), for example, the vital relationship between culture and identity is stressed precisely because it has a significant bearing on attainment. It also engenders the 'compassionate pupil' the book argues for.

Crozier and Davies (2007) focused on a community in the North East of England to verify whether parents of Bangladeshi and Pakistani heritage really are 'hard to reach'. Their research showed that schools can in fact inhibit the participation of minority pupils, even if unintentionally. Regarding pupils' aspirations, of note is their conclusion, following extensive research, that many of the schools 'represente[d] spaces of exclusion' (2007: 311). This was based on what parents, pupils and some teachers said. There was also a lack of concrete evidence highlighting initiatives to engage the parents. The relationship between parents and their children's school thus affects how far parents support academic progress, and is significant when considering pupils' aspirations.

Looking at Crozier and Davies' research, the positioning of parents in relation to the school signifies the level of access they have to help their children academically and bridge the gap between the home and school, particularly when there are several levels of disadvantage at play.

Conceptually, the notions of capital and social reproduction (Bourdieu and Passerson, 1977) are relevant to the way parents' class, social connections and lifestyle directly impact on their and the children's aspirations. Bourdieu formulated concepts about the social hierarchy and the 'cultural capital' required to maintain the status quo and progress within society educationally and economically. While his theory explains only part of what influences a person's social class, opportunities and success, his theoretical framework is widely used to examine wider subjects of structural power and oppression. Authors discussing the educational trajectories of a particular group have commonly used the concept of capital to explain the structural injustices that perpetuate inequalities (Laureau, 1997; Vincent and Martin, 2002; Reay, 1998). Types of capital – social (relating to networks), cultural (relating to the arts, literature, language knowledge), economic (financial capability) – are therefore tenets of the literature that explores the relationship between parents' capital and their children's educational journey. Collectively, these studies explore parents' agency, pointing to the fact that general wellbeing, aspirations and achievement cannot be simplistically mapped onto social class or type of school. Far more complexly woven relationships shape children's schooling – and parents provide a framework that shapes the tapestry.

Enter mothers

So far I have sought in this chapter to establish the legitimacy of including parents in their children's education. It is widely acknowledged by those who specialize in this area that the primary responsibility for a child's welfare is still carried by the mother (Gillies, 2006, 2007; Vincent *et al.*, 2010), even though the 'parent' label suggests neutrality and the equal involvement of both caregivers. Studies have sought to understand the reality for marginalized mothers of various racial backgrounds in the UK (Gillies, 2007), all of whom share the challenges characteristic of the working class: low employability, low family income and partners often working long hours in the service industries. At the other end of the spectrum, middle-classes mothers and their 'intensive mothering'

(Hays, 1996) have been scrutinized for showing how those with resources can sustain the ideal parent persona, fully involved with their children's education and social reproduction (Crozier and Reay, 2005). The marginalization of fathers is a valid and equally necessary story but my study deals only with mothers.

Mothers and intersectionality

The conceptual framework of intersectionality, with its roots in contemporary black feminism, provides a way to understand mothers' experiences. Initially, advocates of the concept argued that along with the gender struggle, women face the simultaneous struggles around race, which intersects gender to give rise to new forms of marginality. Over time, the way numerous axes of marginalization converge in one person – race, gender, class, sexuality, migration and faith, for instance – is used to understand why people see themselves the way they do. When deconstructed, mothers' narratives show how a variety of marginal traits overlap in ways that cannot be captured by one, two or three traditionally defined categories. As Veazey states:

> We need to improve our epistemology of motherhood by understanding how motherhood practices and ideologies are socially and historically constructed and dynamic. Motherhood ideologies and practises are neither static nor universal; they are spatially and temporally dynamic. That is, not only are they different in different times and place, and for different groups of people, they are also capable of being altered through processes such as migration.
>
> (2015: 3)

In other words, motherhood needs to be understood in the specific time and place it happens in and what caused it to come about. I try to take multiple factors into account to refine the knowledge base, the epistemology about motherhood. Such a stance is particularly fitting for Muslim mothers in the UK, who are a wide mix of those born in the United Kingdom, those arriving at a young age and those immigrating as adults. These staggered starting points inevitably influence their trajectories, as do a whole range of other influences. Dynamism is one constant in the discussion on motherhood.

One of many concepts to tackle time and place is 'translocational positionality'. It prioritizes a person's social location (Anthias, 2002), one that is rarely 'fixed' because the layers in our lives are in flux, permeated by time and space in myriad ways. As an exponent of this paradigm, Anthias argues that 'positionality' is particularly relevant to understanding the minority issues of difference and otherness, as:

> This involves looking at both where people are placed within relations of social hierarchy within a time and space framework, and how they position themselves in time and space and in terms of their narrations of their social position in relational terms.
>
> (Anthias, 2011: 213)

Matricentric feminism

> As a framework for interpreting the experiences of mothers, matricentric feminism is consistent with and respectful of the particular, situated realities including the broader familial, social, institutional frameworks in which each mother's life is embedded and her motherwork oriented. Scholars working within this tradition seek to unmask motherhood; they seek to illuminate and articulate a matricentric understanding and appreciation of the diversity and complexity of maternal experiences as well as the commonalities within such experiences.
>
> (Raith *et al.*, 2015: xii)

Since I prioritize the woman's voice in this book, favouring narrative over statistics and grounded theory – see Chapter 3 – over prescriptive frameworks, I must include the personal and acknowledge feminist research. The relationship between feminism and motherhood has a contentious past, as Ribbens observes. At the time she wrote – 1994 – both appeared to be going in different directions and seemed to be accompanied by an ambivalence in women's identities: is motherhood the 'cornerstone of oppression' or a potential position of liberation? For the purpose of setting the context for the rest of my book, I acknowledge, albeit briefly, some key figures, contemporary feminist maternal scholars, in the discussion of motherhood at an intellectual level.

Adrienne Rich, a famous feminist scholar writing about motherhood in the 1970s, broke with all convention in her part-memoire, part intellectual and critical work *Of Woman Born*. The book garnered passionate acceptance and rejection in equal measure. Separating the biological act of mothering and, in Rich's opinion, the 'patriarchal institution of motherhood' (1995: 34) created critical debate, however, becoming the nucleus around which the discipline of maternal scholarship grew in several directions, endorsing, extending or rebuffing Rich's arguments. Andrea O'Reilly (in Abbey and O'Reilly, 1998) brought the identity of motherhood into a central position within feminist thought in the academy. Her contribution of matricentric feminism raised pertinent questions that no discussion on motherhood can ignore, particularly around the legitimacy and value of maternal experience about which there was – up until that point in feminist work – silence. O'Reilly's arguments are not only academic. As director of the Motherhood Initiative for Research and Community Involvement, she translated them into far-reaching activism and publishing work on maternal experience.

In examining what actually takes place in the act of mothering, Sara Ruddick (1989) explored the intellectual activity involved in 'the preservation, growth, and social acceptability' of children (1989: 51), which she defines as a type of work like any other. Ruddick's assertion that the act of 'mothering' can take a variety of shapes, furthers her argument that whoever is a caregiver for the child, investing time and resources should be included as one who 'mothers'. The thrust of her book, however, is about using the motherhood paradigm to negotiate peaceful activism, as opposed to violence, war and destruction.

The fact that Ruddick's classic work focuses on a 'specific discipline of thought – a cluster of metaphysical attitudes, cognitive capacities and values' (1989: 51) – makes it an ideal foundation to justify the need to hear how mothers, particularly those who are marginalized, deal with their children's education. Within maternal scholarship, marginalization on account of ethnicity or race is a site of contention. Black feminists have argued, for example, that white maternal scholarship does not take account of their particular struggles (bell hooks, 1989). For the ensuing narratives in this book, there is much to corroborate this charge. When a further layer – faith, an identifier generally under fire – is added to the mix (as we see in Chapter 2), mothers need to negotiate several levels of relationships, not least that between their own self and their child and between them and their child's school – which is most certainly cerebral work. Ironically, the women who are the subject of this book are caricatured in public opinion as anything but intellectual. Chapter 2 elaborates on how they are perceived and how they see themselves. Suffice to say here, mothers, whether or not they belong to a faith group, are doing intellectual work. If they are not heard in the discourse about children's education, then clearly there is a problem.

Prioritizing the 'mother' figure in scholarly work is not the same as endorsing the 'new momism', which exerts increasing pressure on mothers to raise a 'perfect child', professionalizing the mother's role in unhelpful and unrealistic ways. However, with a growing trend of public discourse judging mothers in every way – from food preparation to 'enrichment' itineraries after school – it is helpful to use Sharon Hays' theoretical framework and her concept of 'intensive mothering' (1996) to understand the nuances of what her mother participants shared in their interviews. This intensive experience is expressed in novel ways, as I show in Chapter 6.

In this chapter, I have attempted to situate families and their relationships with schools. In particular, I have presented a snapshot of the mother's position within research, which shows that until the last 30 to 40 years her identity was wholly unacknowledged. It is an anomaly that while mothers' voices are arguably the most powerful in shaping the future of their children, theirs are the voices least heard in public discourse. In Chapter 2 I deal with the complexity of situating mothers with respect to their faith, and the diversity in their backgrounds and where they live.

Chapter 2
Who and how?

I wanted this space to be for like-minded mothers who shared the same belief system and drew strength and guidance from the same source.

(Latifa)

Before it was Asian family, Asian woman.
Now it's Muslim family, Muslim woman.

(Sonia)

In the previous chapter I touched on aspects of public duty and the positioning of parents and mothers in relation to their children's schools. In particular I established the need for contemporary research to be inclusive of mothers' voices. In this chapter I set out to locate Muslim mothers demographically and spiritually and look at how the media situates them in the public imagination. The key questions I ask are:

- where do Muslim mothers come from demographically?
- what is the position of motherhood as portrayed in Muslim textual sources?
- how do Muslim mothers portray themselves in one public sphere – online?
- how are they projected in the media?

Thinking about any group identity or characteristics poses unending problems. Generalizing about members in one family is misleading; how much more problematic is a faith group. Yet in the public imagination, 'Muslim' is one homogenous label that removes any sense of individuality and difference. When we contextualize mothers in relation to the aforementioned questions, however, we gain some knowledge of their heritage, revealing something of the variety within the most populous Muslim communities in the UK.

So where *exactly*, do you come from?

The common question 'where are you from?' is an inherent part of our daily lives. Sometimes it reveals more about the person asking than the person answering, particularly when an answer such as 'I'm from Leeds' does not satisfy the questioner, who promptly demands: 'but where *exactly* do you come from?' or '... where are your parents from?' This is not necessarily a negative line of questioning. Curiosity is part of what makes us who we are; an interest in another person's background, culture, language, heritage – the exchange and understanding creates a richer experience for us all. Whether someone is from a farming community in the centre of Wales, or has come to the UK from a megacity in India, matters. Each person's narrative has a different context that apart from tangible differences carries esoteric variances: a person's thought patterns, their intonation in speech, their associations, their tastes, their outlook on life. These differences reflect the rich diversity in our world – and ideally would come without value judgements. Where the common values of respect, kindness and humanity prevail, difference is not a threat but an educative experience. We learn from each other. Or rather, we *can* learn from each other.

Fear of differences is where the problem begins on all sides, opening up a dangerous space where difference and similarity mutate into otherness and uniformity. In this space, assumptions, stereotypes, misinformation, lies and sensationalism find fertile ground, take root and spread like ivy.

However one understands the term 'identity', its importance is part of our lives. Unsurprisingly, it appears in expected and unexpected ways in the narratives of the mothers I interviewed. Regardless of how someone asking 'where are you from?' understands identity, the concept itself:

> Offers much more than an obvious, common-sense way of talking about individuality and community. Principally, identity provides a way of understanding the interplay between our subjective experience of the world and the cultural and historical settings in which that fragile subjectivity is formed.
>
> (Gilroy, 1997: 301)

Gilroy's summary of the subtext in the identity question can be understood another way: that two questions are being asked, the first about physical location and heritage and the second about inner orientation, beliefs and ideas. It is this second – inner – location, the one that concerns faith, that forms the common thread unifying the mothers in this book. As this faith identity is the unifying factor – although the level of conviction varies from person to person – it follows that faith-inspired beliefs about motherhood and child birth require some discussion, as a backdrop to the narratives. First, though, I answer the locational question.

Demographic location

The 2011 census provided a snapshot of the Muslim community in England and Wales at that time. It is now well documented that the survey's voluntary question about people's religion has been valuable in gaining a better understanding of the UK's faith communities and general trends regarding religion. The question was completed by 93 per cent of the population.

The document *British Muslims in Numbers* (the data and comparisons draw heavily on the MCB report and are reproduced with kind permission) provides an overview of trends based on the ONS census data and subsequent policy recommendations. Key figures on the whole population of Muslims in England and Wales are presented below.

National identity: 73 per cent of Muslims state that their only national identity is British (or other UK-only identity).

Where do they live? 76 per cent live in the built up, inner city areas of Greater London, West Midlands, the North West and Yorkshire and Humberside. Muslims form 12.4 per cent of London's population. Housing data shows that nearly half of the Muslim population – 1.22 million, or 46 per cent – resides in the 10 per cent most deprived boroughs, an increase of 13 per cent since the 2001 census. By contrast, only 1.7 per cent – 46,000 – live in the 10 per cent least deprived local boroughs (figures are based on the Index of Multiple Deprivation measure).

What's their age profile? 33 per cent of the Muslim population are aged 15 years or under, compared to 19 per cent of the population as a whole. The Muslim population has the youngest age profile out of all the faith groups, with half – or 1.3 million – under the age of 25 years.

How many Muslim children are of school age? 8.1 per cent of all school children in England and Wales – ages 5–15 years – are Muslim. In some inner city London boroughs like Tower Hamlets – where 34.5 per cent of the population is Muslim – Muslim children account for 60 per cent of pupils in schools. Thirty-five per cent of all Muslim married households have dependent children, compared to the national average of 15 per cent. There are 77, 000 – or 10.4 per cent – one-parent families with dependent children.

What is their representation in further education? 24 per cent of Muslims over the age of 16 have 'degree level and above' qualifications, compared to 27 per cent of the general population. Of the 329,694 Muslim full-time students, 43 per cent are female; there are a number of local authorities where the population of Muslim women in full-time education exceeds men. Twenty-six per cent of Muslims identified with the 'no qualifications' category.

What is their employment profile? 29 per cent of Muslim women aged 16–24 are in employment, compared to 50 per cent nationally. Of those in the 16–74 age band, 18 per cent are 'looking after home or family', compared to 6 per cent nationally. Nearly 20 per cent of Muslims are in full-time employment, while 7.2 per cent are unemployed. The respective figures for the overall population are 34.9 per cent and 4.0 per cent.

The figures chosen from the report add an objective context to group identity dynamics, the most obvious of which is diversity – the UK's Muslim population is diverse in every way. Ethnicity and cultural heritage are aspects of diverse identities, which I discuss in Chapter 3 in relation to the participants' profiles. Aside from ethnicity, two other issues form part of the context of the women in this book: health and socio-economic status.

Health

The 2011 census figures show a very young Muslim community. Usually, a younger population would have better health than the rest. Contrary to this expectation, however, the ONS census figures for Muslims reporting 'bad to very bad health' are disproportionately high. In the 50+ age bracket, 24.1 per cent say they fall into this category, as do 38 per cent of Muslim women over 65. By contrast, the respective figures for the national average are 12 and 16 per cent.

Compared to the UK's indigenous population, good health among Muslims over 50 is also less common. This has some bearing on the fact that a higher proportion of Muslim women aged 16 to 74 – three times as many in fact – fulfils a caring role at home as opposed to being in paid work. Similarly, with a very young population of pre-school aged children, more Muslim women are at home raising young children. Research into the link between mental health, poverty and ethnicity (Centre for Social Justice, 2011) makes pertinent points relevant to a holistic understanding of how mothers from minorities fare compared to the rest of the population. Having a cultural heritage from outside the UK has a bearing on several levels – economic activity, higher education take-up, the employment sector and types of jobs done – and, not least, influences whether and how Muslim women do or do not get involved with their children's schools. These links are revisited as they arise in Chapters 4–7.

Socio-economic status

Despite an increase of young people – including Muslim women (43 per cent) – going on to higher education and some closing of the gap in representation at certain levels of occupation – in higher occupations figures for Muslims and the total population stand at 5.5 per cent and 7.6 per cent respectively – Muslims still differ from the rest of population in significant ways. Employment statistics show a relatively high percentage of economic inactivity, for example. This is attributed to the fact that only 30 per cent of students are Muslim, while 31 per cent are looking after children and family (ONS, 2013). Compounding such figures is the fact that a sizeable proportion of Muslims live in deprived areas of low socio-economic status. As such they face similar challenges to other working-class communities. Several studies that take a classed approach have highlighted the experiences of working-class parents regarding their children's education, as we saw in Chapter 1. An intersectional approach looks at other influences that affect employment. Khattab and Johnston's study into what effect an ethno-religious identity has in the labour market is relevant to the context of Muslim mothers. Their data concludes that while there is an employment penalty for most non-white groups in the labour force, within this Muslim men and women face 'greater penalty' than most (Khattab and Johnston, 2014).

Religious and cultural beliefs around caring for elderly parents are another reason why some women, if they can, leave their job to care for parents. Some also take part-time, local work to manage familial responsibilities. This is not too dissimilar to carers in the indigenous population, who do the same. The Joseph Rowntree Foundation report (Khan *et al.*, 2014) examines the barriers being on a low income poses to accessing the labour market. It looks at the challenges faced by three ethnic minority groups in relation to their views and practices around caring for the young and the elderly. The study compared a multitude of issues – ethnicity, childcare options, knowledge of the system – that dissuade people from getting jobs. While it examined the views of Caribbean, Pakistani and Somali parents, most if not all the issues about poverty are relevant when contextualizing the UK's Muslim population.

This sums up the external location the mothers in my research are coming from. In the remainder of the chapter I explore the internal location, the spiritual centre, the commonality that makes such diversity coalesce into a group identity that is neither visible nor quantifiable: Muslim mothers' faith and beliefs.

Motherhood in the Qur'an: Motherhood from the sacred texts

The Qur'an

There is not one monolithic Muslim community in the UK. The Qur'an – which as a word means 'to read' or 'the text which is read' (Haleem, 2010) – is, however, central to a Muslim's belief regardless of which sect they belong to. The basic beliefs, common to the vast majority, are: *tawhid* – or the belief in the Oneness or omnipresence of God; belief in prophethood; belief in the existence of life after death; belief in God's revelations – the Old and New Testaments, the Psalms, the Torah and the Qur'an; and belief in personal accountability in the afterlife. Each of these beliefs is a 'given' and my data shows how they appear throughout the narratives of the mothers I interviewed. The inner world of spiritual conviction, faith and the workings of daily living are bound together for a Muslim, at the centre of which is a commitment to the Qur'an and the life of the last Prophet – Muhammed (*pbuh*).

The Qur'an is believed to have been revealed to the last Prophet of God, Muhammed (*pbuh*), when he reached the age of 40. Verses – ranging from one line to several – were revealed via the angel Gabriel and memorized by the Prophet. These verses were recited to the Prophet's close companions and family, who also memorized what they heard, hence the strong oral tradition of memorizing the text. During the Prophet's lifetime, verses were written by a few scribes – the Prophet himself could neither read nor write – and the Qur'an was recited by the Prophet in its entirety to followers. The verses were primarily about a Muslim's beliefs, in the earliest revelations. *Surahs* – or chapters – consist of a collection of verses varying in length – the shortest chapter consists of one verse, while the longest chapter has 268 verses. Professor Abel Haleem (2010) provides a window into the organization: 'Quantitatively speaking, beliefs occupy by far the larger part of the Qur'an. Morals come next, followed by ritual, and lastly the legal provisions.' Revelation continued for 23 years. Two years after the Prophet's death, the written fragments were compiled in the order the Prophet had instructed during his lifetime, which is believed to be divinely decreed.

Mothers

Motherhood is embedded in several chapters of the Qur'an. It is presented in three ways: first, through vignettes about specific mothers of historic note; second, through the legal contexts such as inheritance laws, marriage and divorce contracts; and third, in terms of mothers' status in the family and social sphere. The concept of motherhood in Islamic primary sources is explored by Schleifer (1996), whose analysis illustrates both the Qur'anic attitude towards the mother as well as her status, rights and obligations. In and amongst verses about women in the Qur'an, there are five stories about mothers. The style in which such stories are told homes in on a few incidents and narrates a close-up view of events, either to correct a misconception – as termed in the Qur'an – or to exemplify a moral and spiritual quality. The five mothers are: Sarah, the first wife of Abraham; the mother of Prophet Moses; Asiyah, Moses' foster mother; Hannah, the mother of Mary and wife of Prophet Imran; and, most significantly, Mary, mother of Jesus, after whom a chapter of the Qur'an is named. Each of these women is shown as an example to those who 'believe', regardless of their gender. Asiyah, the foster mother of Moses and wife of Pharoah – the tyrannical leader of his time – is an example of a woman who retained her beliefs independently, in spite of her husband's well-documented cruelty, which included ordering the death of all Jewish baby boys. Defying his edicts, Asiyah decided to keep and raise the baby boy found afloat on the Nile.

In relation to the same Prophet, Moses, there are several scenes detailing the courage of his biological mother, who was instructed to place her baby in the basket on the Nile and reassured of his safe return to her. The verses describe Moses' mother receiving divine inspiration and the assurance of being reunited with her baby. Woven through the narration of Moses's life – the most mentioned prophet in the Qur'an – is his mother's fortitude and trust in God. This is essentially what a Muslim reader takes away from the story.

Two other mothers – the wife of Prophet Yahya (John), and Hajra (Hagar), the wife of Prophet Ibrahim (Abraham) and mother of Prophet Ismail (Ishmael) – are portrayed as models of patience and courage, the former for praying and waiting for a child, which she is blessed with in old age, and the latter for surviving and conquering the challenge of being left with her baby in the desolate valley of Makkah. It is noteworthy that significant rites performed on the annual Hajj pilgrimage re-enact Hajar's desperate search for water in the valley of Makkah. Year upon year, men and women retrace this mother's footsteps in one of the rites of Hajj. References are also made to the wives of the Prophet Muhammad (*pbuh*) – who are called 'the mothers of the believers' – as timeless spiritual role models to both women and men.

There is no one prescriptive narrative in the Qur'an regarding mothers. There are single mothers, mothers who foster, 'mothers' who are barren, mothers who have babies in old age and the 'mothers of the believers'. The contexts of the vignettes through which we see their lives are faith, integrity, strength – this is what their stories illustrate. The chapter *Maryam*, unlike those detailed above, is far longer and biographical, describing in a detailed narrative Maryam's genealogy, growth and the virgin birth.

Mary

The most notable mother in the Qur'an – and the only one named – is Mary. She forms the title of the nineteenth chapter, *Maryam*. Frame by frame the chapter recounts her birth, genealogy and the virgin birth of Jesus (*pbuh*), emphasizing Mary's position within the 'household of Imran', under the guardianship of Zackariyah. The story about Mary is presented across Chapters 3 and 19. The scholarly thesis by Aliah Schleifer (1997) concludes: 'Her position is not just that of the most exalted category of women, but she is ranked in the highest category of all human beings' (1997: 95), particularly in terms of spiritual development and devotion to the service of God. Schleifer's analysis of the Qur'anic verses and prophetic sayings (*ahadith*) support her argument that 'in no case is Mary seen solely as the mother of Jesus. Rather a reverse attitude tends to prevail. It is the consistent image of Jesus as the son of Mary that remains in mind ...' (1997: 95). What is interesting for Muslims in the central figure of Mary is that there is no contradiction in her being at once a spiritual role model and a mother. Both positions and personas are revered for what they are. As celibacy on an institutional level does not exist in Islam, one of several messages taken from such a detailed narrative as Mary's is her spiritual devotion, of which her motherhood was a part, not the other way round. The figure of Mary is thus a prominent part of the Muslim spiritual psyche.

Aside from the historic accounts of mothers in the Qur'an, its multiple references to motherhood or parenthood regarding social relations are relevant when we peel back the layers of modern-day motherhood to discover where some of its foundations come from.

Mothers are referred to in passages about the identity of parents and their obligations toward their children, particularly at times of contention such as divorce or when managing the rights of orphan children, for instance. From a legal perspective, the discussion about single or divorced mothers emphasizes the need for equity and mercy when negotiating what are usually antagonistic, difficult situations.

The verses in the Qur'an which discuss motherhood/parenthood as a daily lived reality, are explicitly about the adult offspring's responsibility towards both parents, without differing between mothers or fathers, except once. In a verse that calls on respect and compassion for parents, the role of the pregnant mother is elaborated on and elevated. The mother, however, is singled out for greater respect, as in the following verses:

> And we have enjoined on man to be good to his parents: in travail upon travail did his mother bear him, and his weaning is in two years. Show gratitude to Me and to thy parents: to Me is the final goal.
>
> (Luqman 31:14)

> We have enjoined on the human being kindness to his parents; in pain did his mother bear him, and in pain did she give him birth.
>
> (Al Ahqaf, 46:15)

Birth rites

Numerous questions are asked about birth rites by teachers and during general cultural awareness training. The rites of passage are characteristically very simple in Islam. Cultural practices and traditions may clothe the bare bones of a rite of passage, but in essence, all the religious rites of passage have one distinct theme: brevity and the lack of ceremony. So too it is with birth rites. The birth of a baby is noted as a blessing in the Qur'an and an authentic *hadith* tradition, with the birth of a girl emphasized as an additional blessing: "Whoever takes care of two girls until they reach adulthood, he and I will come (together) on the Day of Resurrection" (saying of Prophet Muhammad – *pbuh*). The birth of a child is free of sin – whether a girl or a boy, children are born in a state of innocence and purity, with no blame or guilt associated with their existence. The mother's pregnancy, delivery and breast-feeding are enumerated amongst the highest 'spiritual station[s]' a person achieves.

Soon after the baby is born, the first tradition is to whisper the call to prayer in their right ear. This call testifies to bearing witness to One God, and to Prophet Muhammad as the Messenger of God. It is the same call to prayer as that from mosques around the world, marking the times of the five daily prayers. Charity is given as an expression of gratitude, which takes the shape of providing food for orphans or those in need. This act of charity and naming the child is known as *aqiqah*. A celebratory gathering of friends and family is a commonly known as an *aqiqah* party, where gifts are given for the newborn.

What impact has this had on modern-day parenting, and specifically mothering? Over the past 30 years there has been unprecedented movement of Muslim people to other parts of the world. A dislocated, moving global community, uprooted from their cultural heritage and planting lives in new lands, has stimulated the increased publication of Muslim parenting books for a European and North American readership. To some extent the recent literature testifies to holding onto a 'Muslim' identity when so many communities are transient. The main thrust of these books are discussions on contemporary issues infused with the gold standards of Muslim parenting: to provide a spiritual, God-centred environment for one's children, where manners, family and social relations are a few of the many virtues extolled. Well-known advice these books reiterate is the oft-quoted *hadith*: 'The best thing a parent can give their children is manners.' Woven together, these elements come under the umbrella term *tarbiyah* – translated as 'upbringing and education'. There is no distinction in the Islamic classical texts that discuss *tarbiyah*, between learning algebra or grammar and learning manners – they were all one and the same.

From this bird's-eye view of Muslim parents' landmark concerns comes the mindset of generations of Muslim mothers, conscious of their spiritual status as a mother and to their joint responsibility for the *tarbiyah* of their child. Time and geography have no doubt produced countless permutations, infused and extracted, yielding not one but several 'motherhoods'. How far any of these elements have tapped into contemporary mothers' views and ways of thinking about education, is the question I consider next.

How Muslim mothers position themselves online

Against the textual backdrop, a look at how contemporary Muslim mothers are positioning themselves may give the reader some insight into how their thought processes, life choices, concerns and interests with regards to mothering have developed over time – notwithstanding the changeability in time and place. The legitimacy of exploring how mothers are positioning themselves online fits with a growing body of research into religious identities online. Anne Piela's study, for example, covered a broad network of online discussion groups, unearthing both the subject matter Muslim women discussed – such as marriage and sexuality, gender roles and work – and the *way* they went about their discussions, using Qur'anic evidence and *ahadith* for their diverse interpretations and various points of reference.

Piela argues for the need to research Muslim women's online voices as a counter narrative to:

> Remove the imbalance which exists in the representations of their experience. The fact that 'ordinary', non-academic Muslim women discuss Islam online indicates that an independent quest for knowledge has become a common way of obtaining an Islamic education. This shapes their perceptions of who they are online and off.
>
> (Piela, 2012)

There is a curious binary at play in sharing mothers' online activity: doing so excludes those who do not use online resources but ignoring such activity for this reason limits the reader's access to a valuable source. I have included the discussion here not to replace but rather to complement the data from the face-to-face interviews.

Researching Muslim *mothers'* groups and forums online – as opposed to Muslim *women's* – throws up certain patterns in their interests and concerns, which they voice in forums, blogs and on social media pages. There is an abundance of sites about education and sites about faith and spirituality, social empowerment and fashion, clothing and food. In addition there is a growing Muslim marriage and relationship community, in pursuit of the right match. Websites that are clearly for Muslim mothers offer resources on parenting, education, Islamic studies, family relationships and faith-specific subjects, such as daily acts of worship – like the five Prayers – or ideas and resources around festivals such as Eid and Hajj. This is not that different to what other mothers are involved in online, as a look at well-known UK site Mumsnet will show. Other sites popular across faiths and ethnicities include educational sites – specifically those that relate to home schooling, health and extra-curricular activities.

One particular group of mothers – who I present here – illustrates the ways mothers scaffold their identities, interests and concerns on a virtual platform. The following case study material is provided by the founder – Latifa – and one of the five administrators, Razia, of Muslim Mamas. Both women are in their early 30s, care for their children full time and combine part-time work – Latifa in the social services sector and Razia in education project management – with long-term commitments in the voluntary sector. Their case studies present their narratives in response to the following questions:

- how did the Muslim Mamas page start?
- what would you say, from the page interactions, are top concerns of Muslim mothers generally?
- what do you find the page (the MM closed group of over 8000 members) is most commonly used for?
- what are the school concerns mothers have raised most on the closed group?
- what do you think differentiates it from any other mothers' page or online forum?

Muslim Mamas

Muslim Mamas is the designated name of the Facebook group, used here with permission of the group's founder. They bring the number of participants in my research to 53.

> Latifa: Muslim Mamas was set up on 10 January 2011. It was this photo of my son sleeping face down with his bottom up in the air that launched our internet group of mums, a second family as so many call it. I posted this photo up on my profile in exasperation and bemusement after many sleepless nights. I felt the need to share this moment and was trying to reach out, make a connection, with someone, anyone, who knew and felt the same as me. Unexpectedly, many of my friends responded and commented about their own children's sleeping habits and their own experiences. They shared that moment with me. My heart sighed and smiled in relief. Suddenly, being a first time mum didn't feel so lonely anymore. My experience was shared. I was not alone. I had a community, a sisterhood, right at my fingertips. That's when I thought that there's a wealth of knowledge and experience to draw on, support to be had for all of us mothers and that there needs to be a bank/pool/forum to share it in, freely and openly. It was then that I created the group 'Manic Mums' (later renamed Muslim Mamas).
>
> I wanted this space to be for like-minded mothers who shared the same belief system and drew strength and guidance from the same source. To not just strive and learn together to be better mothers but also better Muslims. I felt this solidified the bond we had and immediately gave us a common ground. The group

literally exploded. By the end of the first week, I had over 500 members. Within a month, it shot to over 1000.

As the group expanded so rapidly, I set up more subgroups which were equally popular. Most importantly, I struck gold. The gold I found was my invaluable admin team, all of whom I met on Muslim Mamas! These ladies are my rock and they share the same vision as me as to what MM stands for.

We made the decision to change the groups to a secret setting in order to tame the flow of join requests. Muslim Mamas is what we like to call a 'hijab-free' zone where there are no men allowed and we can all let out hair down and have a cuppa together. That's how we envisage it anyway.

Alhamdulillah (All praise is due to God alone), almost five years on, here we are now at over 8000 members, 9 groups, 1 Facebook page with 20k followers. We have a few plans in the pipeline *inshaAllah* (God Willing) and really want to continue this service in the hope that it will benefit many other mothers feeling just as exasperated as I did that day I posted that photo of my son.

Muslim Mamas is an international platform, we have members from all over the world *mashaAllah*. It really helps connect us to mothers who we may never have otherwise met, experience cultures we may never have experienced. However, it is essentially a UK-based forum as all the administrators are from the UK, mostly London. In terms of age, again it is a variety but certainly those who comment more are in their twenties or thirties.

SD: What do you think differentiates it from any other 'mothers' page or online forum?

Razia: In my opinion, the stringent vetting process to ensure our mums are 'safe' and feel confident to share things on such an intimate platform, is something special. There have been many other copy-cat groups but none that have organically grown as rapidly as we have; we became a secret group as we could not cope with the sheer number of join requests. Our group also boasts of varied and many well-known Muslim personalities from authors, journalists, businesswomen, artists, motivational speakers, counsellors, educators, craft-makers, chefs and last but not least bakers, including Britain's national sweetheart Nadiya

Hussain! What is most inspirational about Muslim Mamas is the ambition that Mamas hold. In front of our very eyes, we have seen our own Mamas go on to do wonderful things, attaining celebrity status such as Halima Saleem, founder of 'Curry On Halima'. Admin also runs a very tight ship in terms of managing conflicts, negative language etc. We try to keep the group upbeat, positive, inspiring our Muslim mamas to be ambassadors of Islam.

Latifa: The beauty of these groups is how sisters pool together and support each other. We share joys as well as sorrows together. We may have heated discussions but we try to learn from one another.

SD: What do you find the member-only page is most commonly used for?

Razia: Faith-wise it's mainly *fiqh* (legal) questions such as etiquette of prayer, hijab, Islamophobia, different schools of thought, marital duties, bringing children up etc.

Culturally, it's in-laws and subsequent duties towards them, how to cope with husbands from 'back home', cultural clashes with reverts etc.

There's lots of children/baby-related posts seeking general advice, lots of health advice and requests for prayers, quite a few tongue-in-cheek posts where Mamas share their sense of humour, games to get mamas involved, current affairs news, personal photos and of course our themed 'Open Sundays' where they share their personal photos based on a theme. We also aim to hold a monthly clinic on various relevant topics such as *Zakat*, led by an expert in the field or an evening with a current personality such as former BBC's *The Apprentice* candidate Nurun giving business advice. We decide the topic based around what our Mama's are experiencing at the time or if we notice a topic Mamas are asking about frequently.

SD: What are the top few topics that recur generally, and what are the most popular education-related subjects discussed?

Latifa: Children, pregnancy and babies (including matters like vaccination), education/schooling, marital issues.

Razia: Which schools to apply to, bullying in schools, how to support children's learning etc.

> Latifa: Home schooling has been a big topic since the group started. It is still a hot topic and this usually stems from disillusionment in the National Curriculum or disillusionment with schools.

The need for a commonality beyond the status and work of mothering is significant here. It shows that the 8000 women who have made the decision to become members are concerned about their role as Muslim mothers and the implications of making choices based on their faith as part of their lives. The same commonality was found in Piela's (2011) much wider study of online communication:

> There is an important element of interaction and collaboration in these discussions—agreements, disagreements, comments and references to other members' postings shape a dynamic environment that facilitates collaborative readings of Islam. The opportunity to engage with other religiously framed viewpoints, as many participants admitted, improved their understanding of Islam and bonded them to other Muslim sisters.
>
> (2011: 263)

Apart from the difference in technological facilities, the mothers in Piela's research position themselves in stark contrast to their mothers' generation, whose identities were firmly rooted in ethnic and cultural positions.

As participating mothers in this group, the Muslim Mamas' independent discussions challenge several essentialized versions of a 'Muslim woman and mother'. There are posts about the division of labour between working husbands and wives and the expectation of mothers and fathers sharing responsibility for raising children. The woman also share their concerns, navigating them in their own way. And in seeking solutions, it is common to see them reference the Qur'an and *hadiths* to explain certain viewpoints or when they are offering advice. Because of the cultural diversity of the mothers' membership – Muslim Mamas come from around the globe – a frequent subject of discussion is non-Muslim family members and engendering good relationships with them. This might be because the type of mother who joins the group is one who subscribes to a faith-centred view. That being said, having participated online the commitment to faith is clearly varied – mothers in the group use 'Muslim' as loosely or deeply as they choose.

Muslim mothers in the media

The brief example of the Muslim Mamas illustrates the way mothers are organizing themselves online, constructing their collective identity. If race and culture were the identifiers 20 years ago, much has happened – too complex to discuss here – that has resulted in a multi-ethnic group coming together under a spiritual, faith label. If we look at the shift in public discourse – in the media, for example – from an 'Asian' identity to a 'Muslim' one, we can see that today's society now favours a faith identity above an ethnic identity. How one locates the starting point in this knotted ball of string is the subject of specialist works. To enrich the context of Muslim mothers, as this chapter sets out to do, a final look at one specific area is required: how *they* are situated in the media. Within the tomes of study on the portrayal of Muslims in the media, Muslim mothers are again in a curious position – present through their absence.

Who is portrayed, how they are re-presented and why their stories enter the media space are far-reaching questions that warrant a study in their own right. Who is left out, and where and how a void exists, is equally worthy of attention. A number of recent studies have analysed how Muslims in the UK are presented. The study by Baker *et al.* (2012) at the University of Lancaster, for example, analysed over 200,000 articles from 1998 to 2009, looking at the wording most commonly associated with Muslims and the content most frequently discussed. It concluded that:

> The representations of Muslims we found in the British press ranged from those that were intended to be antagonistic to more subtle, possibly unconscious practices which constructed Muslims as similar to each other and different from 'westerners', engaged in conflict or likely to hold extremist views.
>
> (Baker *et al.*, 2012: 12)

Gabrielatos and McEnery found that much less tabloid and broadsheet space was given to articles on everyday matters such as education, food, travel, family and general interest. Yet print media stories alone are only part of the complex tapestry of how Muslims are defined in the public imagination. Gaine and Lamley (2003) contribute a pertinent angle to the study of media narratives: 'It is too simplistic to blame the media: the interplay between the media and politicians and their joint construction of news are what generates new race agendas and concerns' (2003: 9).

Muslim women are depicted in one of three ways; as victims of FGM, forced marriage and other forms of oppression, in terms of their clothing – the hijab or niqab – or as potential threats to national security as extremists. That it is true that there are injustices and social ills that urgently require addressing is not being disputed; abuse of anyone in society, regardless of gender or race, is worthy of attention and commentary, especially if it is a growing trend. The problems of FGM, honour killings and forced marriages all have roots in certain cultures that cannot be grafted onto 'Islam', a faith which neither advocates nor legitimizes such crimes. What constitutes a valid marriage in Islam is discussed in Chapter 5. As for the obsession with the hijab/niqab in the press, the politicization of these items of clothing – the latter of which is worn by a tiny fraction of Muslim women – has taken attention away from far more important issues such as employment, health, higher education and the economic status of the women.

While these issues surface with predictable frequency, the 'Muslim woman extremist' trope is the latest and possibly most damaging stone to be thrown. Over the last decade a combination of selective images, inflammatory headlines and stories have combined to ensure that the Muslim woman is seen by the public as a figure of threat, self-segregating and directly opposing the wellbeing of the general population. In terms of extremism, they are seen as both perpetrators of crimes and the parent responsible for monitoring and subsequently preventing extremism in their young adult children – 'Muslim Mothers should be trained in computing "to help spot radicalisation"' (*The Independent*, 2014). Analysing the portrayal in the media of Asian British Muslim women specifically, Bhimji concludes: 'The hegemonic media thus fails to take into account the diversity and plurality of British Asian Women' (Bhimji, 2012: 50).

In the popular media Muslim mothers have been the subject of contradictory headlines, labelled everything from the barbaric – they pose security threats to passive, oppressed bystanders (Hughes, 2016) – to the dysfunctional – they have 'insufficient command of the English language' (Hughes, 2016). In spite of adjusting the lens, the dire picture remains much the same: Muslim women are alien, othered and dehumanized.

This brief look at how Muslims have been depicted in the media in the last 15 years shows Muslim mothers portrayed within a limited framework of oppression, and economic and educational inactivity. More recently, they have been characterized as both victims and perpetrators of extremism: a double-sided oppositional narrative.

En route to meeting the participants in my study in Chapter 3, this chapter has aimed firstly to contextualize their external reality by casting a glance at their demographics, and secondly, to locate their spiritual side via a pit-stop of the relevant parts of their sacred primary source texts. The case study of the founders of the Muslim Mamas Facebook group provided a bridge to Muslim mothers' contemporary self-representation online, before I offered a brief assessment of how mothers are positioned in the national press. Conversations without context themselves add to the polarized views and experiences I attempt to harness in this book.

In the next chapter, I look at the specific characteristics of the mothers' ethnicity and where they live in relation to the rationale and methods for the way my research was conducted. As the themes in the book rely on the mothers' accounts, I explore the ethical challenges in the process of 're'-searching these accounts to provide a window into rooms where doors would otherwise be firmly shut. Hence Chapter 3, although respectful of conventions about discussing research, is equally a view onto lives and experiences, prioritizing the 'home' in the home–school binary.

Hide and seek
The re-searched and the searcher

Can you tell them private school fees are too high. Thanks sis.

(Saira)

Do you have children, how old are they?

(Kausar)

Have you felt it? That atmosphere before the governing body meeting starts?

(Tahira)

In this chapter I introduce and contextualize the 53 participant mothers. I consider the process of interviewing them and explore the ethical issues of how a person positions themselves in relation to those they are researching.

Our interactions with each other are masked. Different parts of ourselves interact in a range of ways depending on who we are communicating with and where. There is a vast space between our inner selves and the way we choose to project ourselves. We hide one persona to present another that we judge to be relevant to the situation, and – simultaneously – we seek facets of another person, facets they may or may not reveal depending on what they hide and what they seek. This dualism is keenly felt in the qualitative research process – it is nuanced and subtle; hide and seek.

Seeing the research process in this light allowed me to accept the subjectivity of speaking to another person about their experience. At its most basic level, that is what my research meant to me.

Methodology
Unlike research that sets out to solve a particular problem or test a hypothesis, my aim was to contribute voices to the space in public discourse so sparsely occupied with real experiences around parents from marginal groups. I therefore adopted the qualitative approach using methods such as interviewing, focus groups and observation to give my participants a fuller opportunity to express their experience, particularly, as Rubin and Rubin (2012) state, 'when the processes being studied are nearly invisible' (p. 5).

Interviewing is also the best way of getting to grips with people's subjective reality – how they understand their experience from where they stand. In particular I used the naturalist approach to interviewing, which was well suited to the needs of the project, allowing participants to share the often complex mix of what they experienced. Rubin and Rubin (2012) state that: 'Depth implies examining layers of meaning, gradually unpeeling the onion to get at the heart of the matter' (2012: 103).

Another way to look at interviewing is to see the responses as narratives, 'to empower the respondent to set the agenda' (Elliot, 2005: 23). This perspective resonated with my aims, particularly in light of the group of women I planned to approach and why. Goodall (2008) validates the importance of narratives, encapsulating the relationship between them, interviewing and the participants thus: 'At the heart of interviewing research is an interest in other individuals' stories because they are of worth' (2008: 5).

The research process requires being explicit about the theories one aligns oneself to. I took a constructivist grounded theory approach, which essentially means two things. First, the approach sees reality as socially constructed, affected by the researcher, the participants, the location and historic factors (Charmaz, 2008). Second, grounded theory advocates going into the 'field' and generating theory from participants' data, as opposed to going into the field with a theory and testing it. The original tenets of grounded theory involved the 'general method of comparative analysis' (Glaser and Strauss, 1967: 1) whereby data generated is concurrently analysed and compared. This influences the next stage of data generation, which again undergoes analysis. While this has evolved and been modified over time by second- and third-generation grounded theorists, I discuss only elements – the positionality of the participants, accepting the researcher's subjectivity and the mutual construction of data, for instance – that are relevant to my research. I follow Charmaz regarding the way themes and categories are found from the participants' narratives: 'When we seek to learn how people construct meanings, we can discover which meanings they hold and how these meanings might answer the question of what our emerging category is about' (2008: 144).

My rationale for taking this constructivist approach developed organically as the purpose of the research gradually evolved – primarily to hear how a pivotal group in society sees and understands their reality. Although the approach only emerged in the second generation of grounded theorists, its emphasis on understanding participants in relation to their social construct seems best suited to gauge reasons for a particular way of thinking. The participants are understood in relation to their background, physical context and how these affect the way *they* make meaning of their lives. This drives the research (Mirza, 1998). Using grounded theory means being open to themes that emerge from the interviews which may not necessarily fit familiar discourses. I approached the research as a way of capturing the participants' realities: their ways of experiencing and being, negotiating and navigating beyond conventional notions.

Research context and participants

Individuals cannot represent a group; any label given to a group will be contested. With this in mind, I sought out participants who, whilst not representative of Muslim mothers per se, were loosely related to the broad categories in the 2011 census, namely: ethnicity, geographic location and socio-economic status. I sought to present both a wide selection of mothers and those who corresponded to the largest groups of Muslims in the census data.

Timing and sampling

I sent the gatekeepers information on my rationale for the project and made clear my ethical position about participants' anonymity and confidentiality. If individual interviews were difficult to arrange in a particular location, the gatekeepers recruited focus group participants. A similar guide to that used in the interviews was used for the focus group discussions. The benefits of this, as rationalized by Morgan, make the case for the approach: 'Less structured groups are most useful for exploratory purposes. Listening to what the participants choose to discuss in a less structured group reveals their perspective on the research topic' (Morgan, 1998: 47).

The final tool I used was 'memoing' – a means of recording 'internal dialogue' from the initial stages of conceiving the research topic (Birks and Mills, 2015). Used as a device to record activities, map connections and reflect, this method facilitated an organic relationship between the research process, data generation and analysis.

Individual interviews were held with 24 of the 53 mothers, and 27 participated in focus groups. Three mothers – one from each focus group – were interviewed individually, hence the increase in the total number of participant interactions. At the beginning of each interview, I handed my interviewee a leaflet outlining what was going to happen and some common questions. All the participants signed an individual consent form.

When necessary, I translated key parts of the leaflet and consent form into spoken Urdu and Bengali. In the focus group with the Somali mothers, the gatekeeper translated the key information at the beginning of the meeting and explained the purpose of the consent form, before asking the participants if they agreed and would sign it.

Five participants had interviews that went beyond discussing their personal experience with schools. These were conducted to talk about the dynamics of their local community in relation to education. They afforded the women the opportunity to share their professional experience either working with mothers in the public sector or as school staff. Desk research and an online case study – as presented in Chapter 2 – also informed the research, in an attempt to delve for both width and depth in the mothers' voices and experiences.

The research was scheduled for the summer term 2015 and due to finish before the start of Ramadan. I knew participants would be unlikely to take on such a commitment at that time, given the increased spiritual and communal activities during the month of fasting and prayer. I chose term time specifically to minimize the pressures of childcare and because it allowed me to conduct the focus groups in school settings.

Location

Selecting participants on the basis of location used the data from the 2011 census, which showed the most populated areas by religion and ethnicity. A second consideration was the practical matter of where gatekeepers were located. When I compared the key locations to my personal network, I found a good enough correlation to obviate the need for any further participants.

The sampling purposely took account of socio-economic status, education level, job status and ethnicity to ensure a wide spectrum of participants. This comes with a caveat: in two locations, I had no idea who would arrive for the focus groups. The invitations were left to the discretion of the gatekeepers, who had read what I had written to familiarize themselves with the purpose of the research.

I wrote information leaflets to colleagues in the voluntary sector, or acquaintances I had been introduced to through our common interest in social work, minorities and education. The leaflet explained the purpose of the research, and why I was searching for a diverse representation of Muslim mothers. There was, however, no mention of denominations, as this aspect of their faith has little bearing on their relationship with their child's school. Such efforts yielded a diverse mix of mothers, who took part in either interviews or focus groups:

Location 1: 7 individual interviews

Location 2: 1 focus group (13 participants) and 1 individual interview (3 participants participated in a focus group and individual interview)

Location 3: 1 focus group (7 participants) and 3 individual interviews

Location 4: 1 focus group (4 participants) and 1 individual interview

Location 5: 17 individual interviews

Individual interviews = 29

Focus group participants = 24

The gatekeepers were pivotal in speaking to the groups of mothers who either attended or worked in their institution. They organized a time and date with the mothers (or accommodated our focus group) in one of their regular meetings. This recruited participants efficiently and quickly. Within term time, mothers who were not in employment were interviewed during schools hours. Those in full-time and part-time work I interviewed on evenings and weekends. The focus groups that met in schools were conducted on the premises. These and most of the individual interviews were held between April and June, though a few interviews took place in the autumn term. The locations were as follows:

Location 1: A centre for minority-ethnic women in a metropolitan district of Yorkshire, one of the most densely populated areas of the UK. The women come into the centre for language support, parenting, health and family advice. The multi-ethnic, multilingual, all-woman team provides a range of services to girls and women, generally from the deprived surrounding areas. The mothers interviewed were service providers; their educational qualifications ranged from GCSE to postgraduate level. Their ethnicities included Bangladeshi, Pakistani and Arab. Three were service users.

Location 2: A parents' weekly coffee morning group in a primary school, consisting of mothers who live in inner city East London. The school, rated by Ofsted as 'good' (2014), has an intake of mainly Bangladeshi pupils and is larger than the average primary school. Just over half of its pupils are eligible for free school meals, and in 2014, 93 per cent and 95 per cent attained a Level 4 and above in English – for writing and reading respectively – while 90 per cent achieved a Level 4 and above in mathematics. The highest educational achievement for half of the mothers here was completing compulsory schooling in the UK or Bangladesh. Several had also completed vocational courses in further education institutions.

Location 3: A group of mothers at a primary school in West London, rated 'good'. Situated on a housing estate with a diverse population, the school has four times more pupils with English as an additional language than the average primary school in England. Sixty-three per cent are also eligible for free school meals. In 2014, 88 per cent attained a Level 4 and above in Maths and 79 per cent achieved a Level 4 and above in English at the end of Key Stage 2 tests. All the mothers in the group were of Somali heritage. Their education varied from partial to full completion of secondary education in Somalia. Half attended English language courses and one was pursuing a route into higher education.

Location 4: A women's study group, run in a participant's house, in a suburb in an ethnically mixed city in the East Midlands. The mothers were either of British Pakistani or British Indian heritage. Two were graduates, two were in part-time work and was one combining study with work. All of the mothers held voluntary roles of responsibility within local schools or had done so in the past.

Location 5: Participants here were from a diverse, densely populated nonmetropolitan town in a county in the South East of England. Some had no education at all while others had degrees. Over half were in full-time work and a quarter were in part-time work. Their ethnicities included, in descending order: Pakistani, Arab, English, Indian and Bangladeshi. One-third had no qualifications and two-thirds were graduates, three with postgraduate qualifications. Their children attended a range of primary schools, which fell into two categories – Type A and Type B.

Type A: These schools were smaller than the average size with less than 20 per cent of pupils from ethnic minorities. They also had few disadvantaged pupils, with just below 3 per cent eligible for free school meals. The schools achieved above the national average in English and Maths at Key Stage 1 and 2, and on average 4 per cent of their children had Special Educational Needs (SEN), including those on 'action plus', which brings a stream of extra funding for educational support.

Type B: Such schools were much larger than the average primary school and the percentage of children eligible for free school meals ranged from 22–39 per cent. On average, 8 per cent of pupils had SEN or were on action plus and required support. In 2014 Key Stage 2 results for English and Maths at Level 4 were 75 per cent and 85 per cent respectively. Both were just below the national average. Although these schools have made improvements in their attendance records, their attendance figures are still among the lowest 20 per cent nationally.

Challenges

The focus groups varied in size, composition and location. The 13 mothers in the largest group (in location 2) required additional help to manage late entrances and early departures. A few young children also accompanied their mothers. The school family liaison officer gave welcome support. The gatekeeper who first made contact with the group could not be there when they arrived, but her prior communication ensured that all the women – and a few unexpected arrivals – turned up on time and were ready to be part of a group discussion. The dynamics between the vocal and more reticent members of the group had to be carefully handled at times. It also required techniques to draw in those who did not contribute whilst simultaneously stemming the tide of the dominant's views and anecdotes. It was important to be attentive to 'multi-dimensional performances in our research site', where silence needs to be probed, to 'elicit those narratives that have previously gone unnamed, unnoticed, unthought' (Mazzei, 2008: 52).

The focus groups in locations 3 and 4 presented different challenges. The former required the gatekeeper to translate for half of those who did not speak English, which slowed the interactions down so they took almost twice as much time as we had originally planned.

About 6–8 participants were expected in location 4. Because of appointments, altered work shifts and children's ill-health, only five eventually arrived and one was available for an individual interview after the group discussion. Again, due to the diligence of the gatekeeper, the participants already had a grasp of what the research was about and two had thought in advance about the points they wanted to raise. The gatekeepers were of immense help in allocating a secure, private space for me to conduct the interviews and the focus groups.

Ethical considerations

Early on in the research design I decided not to interview participants in their own homes in case it was culturally insensitive. For example, an elderly member of their family might expect to be included in our 'conversation' – as they would see it – which would have affected the confidentiality, fluency and subject matter covered. Only one mother was interviewed in her home, as she could guarantee that no other family members would be present.

Several mothers, before, during and after the interviews, asked me practical questions about their children's education. Although this raised an ethical issue, I decided that helping them was in the spirit of our exchange in that I believed it should benefit them too. I also reasoned that the advice or information they sought was not related to anything sensitive or confidential, nor did it affect their answers during the interview. The type of questions they asked, for example, were: where do I go for information about Adult Learning courses? How do I make an appointment to have a meeting with a headteacher? Tell me about accredited ESOL levels. Oakley's (1981) critical exploration of interview methodology raises several ethical dilemmas when interviewing mothers. Much of her experience of the research process as interactive and rapport building resonated with my experiences, as did her criticism of the contemporary 'textbook paradigms', which ignore emotions. An unexpected benefit of the interviews was the repeated feedback after their completion that the mothers felt they had personally benefitted from the reflective experience of thinking about their journey as a parent with regards to their child's schooling.

Employment status

Twenty-two out of the 51 mothers were not in paid work and approximately half were pursuing studies in various settings and over different time periods and levels. Their efforts to further their education ranged from doctoral studies, Learning Support Assistant courses and ESOL classes to short, school-based courses to improve maths, literacy and parenting. Because English classes and short school-based courses are transitory, I could not gather accurate figures for attendees.

Participants' work status was never explicitly sought by the gatekeepers so I only found out whether someone was in paid employment or not at interview, when I asked for brief biographical information, which I then recorded onto a grid.

I also tried to ascertain other factors: who was in full-time paid work, who was in part-time work and who was devoted to caring roles at home, for example. The following gives a snapshot of the participants' status at the time of the interviews. Most of the mothers – 47 out of the 51 – were married, three were single and one was a widow. Their ages ranged from 29 to 47. The number of children they had and whether they were in early years, primary or secondary school (or higher education) significantly affected the mothers' interactions. Only two had a single child, 12 had four or more (maximum six), so the average number was three.

Interestingly, employment status didn't necessarily correlate with common assumptions and categories about class. The construction of working, middle and upper classes is itself debateable, but if we take these categories as they are understood in everyday terms, it would still be difficult to categorize these women, especially as almost half were not born in the UK and the process of immigration destabilizes convenient classifications. What is relevant to my study, however, is the variety of full-time, part-time and unpaid work the mothers are doing alongside mothering. Their social and geographical locations were varied too, as can be deduced from the data and sites of interviewing. At the very least, diversity contributes to the body of research that breaks the 'cultural circles' Ribbens (1994: 12) identifies. Ribbens argues that middle-class researchers discuss the views of middle-class mothers, addressing a middle-class elite in institutions that might all reinforce each other's views. This consequently pathologizes working-class child rearing.

Ethnicity: Roots and routes

Taking an aerial view of the UK's Muslim population does not allow for the huge variety of cultures, heritages and the differences between them. Ethnicity as a concept is not as neat as the box one ticks on a form. As Gaine and Lamley caution: 'ethnicity is not fixed, especially at the margins' (2003: 78). This rings particularly true when one lives as a second- or third-generation ethnic minority. Each generation combines cultural roots and contemporary lifestyles in innovative and far from static ways.

Significantly, at the time of the 2011 census just under half – 47 per cent – of the Muslim population were born in the UK. The rest were born in Africa, the Middle East, Asia and Europe. The Muslim population's changing constitution can be explained in various ways. The report from the Muslim Council of Britain sheds light on where migrants are coming from:

> About 20% of the increase in the Muslim population can be attributed to the 'Other Asian' and 'Other Black' ethnicity categories, the former reflecting settlement from Sri Lanka and Afghanistan, both areas of conflict. There has also been a significant rise in the Somali Muslim population in the last decade, but in the absence of a specific ethnic category, it is not possible to provide a definitive figure.
>
> (Sundas, 2015: 24)

The 2011 census figures show that the largest ethnic group in the Muslim community is 'Asian': 68 per cent of the Muslim population is either Pakistani, Bangladeshi, Indian and 'other Asian' – for example, Sri-Lankan. The second and third largest ethnic groups – 7.2 and 6.6 per cent respectively – are of

African and Arab heritage. Amongst these, some background information about the two larger groups will help add essential context.

Heritage of the mothers in the study

South Asian origin

Of the 51 mothers in the study, 37 are of Pakistani and Bangladeshi heritage, and thus reflect the largest group in the census. The erroneous notion that Asians are all the same still persists. The history of the Asian subcontinent is complex. This isn't helped by the fact that a school can have over 20 ethnicities in it, which makes 'global schools' take on a whole new meaning. Chris Gaine uses the example of Pakistanis to illustrate this point:

> There are many significant differences between Indians, Bangladeshis and Pakistanis in Britain, but they are often described as the ethnic group Asians. Indeed there are significant differences within these three national categories. In Pakistan, there are four regional ethnic groups: Punjabis, Pushtuns, Sindhis, and Baluchis.
>
> (Gaine and Lamley, 2003: 77)

As Gaine rightly observes, however: 'In Britain they become Asian, grouped together with Bangladeshis, whose roots are a thousand miles further east, and other Indians who speak yet another language and practise another religion' (Gaine and Lamley, 2003). While the geographical differences are less marked for second- and third-generation Asians in the UK, with over half the Muslim population born overseas the cultural influences and issues that come with migration remain significant for new migrants. Migration itself requires a tremendous negotiating of identity as people cross cultural, political and geographical boundaries. All three groups – Indian, Pakistani and Bangladeshi – have a long history of settlement in the UK, going back to the late 19th century. Several publications, keen to preserve the early history of arrival from the Indian subcontinent, depict how these communities evolved.

In Chapter 1 I mentioned several studies that look at regional, generational and identity issues, which help contextualize the mothers in my research. Pakistani communities are concentrated in northern towns such as Bradford and in Birmingham in the Midlands, while East London is home to the largest Bangladeshi population. The 2011 census data, however, shows some movement away by Pakistanis and Bangladeshis from such concentrated communities to more diverse areas. Nonetheless, there are still significant communities such as the Mirpuri, who live in Bradford, Birmingham and pockets of the Home Counties. These communities were historically reputed to be introverted and self-segregating, marrying and socializing only within their communities and deeming others from the same country of origin outsiders. Their segregation is not solely on ethnic grounds either but also culturally specific to their community. The same is true of the Sylheti community in parts of East London, though again not all people choose to stay within that community. There is a pattern in their demographics too – extended families live near each other as a matter of convenience. Such arrangements make their daily living more challenging in some ways, heightening their obligations towards relatives. At the same time, however, they receive help from relatives for childcare and share responsibility for their children's upbringing.

Somali origin

The UK's British-Somali population has grown significantly in the last 30 years. The Somali community has had a presence here since the late 19th century but more recently more people from Somalia arrive in flight from civil war or move from other European, particularly Scandinavian, countries. The first arrivals in the 1950s were Somali men employed as merchant seamen, who settled in Cardiff, Manchester, Birmingham and Sheffield (Change Institute, 2009). Later arrivals settled in London during the 1980s and 1990s. Depending on where and how data is gathered, estimates about the population living in the UK vary. There was no 'Somali' category (Open Society, 2014) in the 2011 census so estimates are taken from the country of birth data and range. This varies from 99,484 (Census, 2011) to 250,000 (Sundas, 2015: 24).

Civil war and disturbance in Somalia saw many Somalis seek asylum in the UK directly. Others spent time in refugee camps in neighbouring countries en route. Significant numbers of 'secondary' arrivals came later, having tried to settle in other European countries, mainly those in Scandinavia or Holland. The profile of Somalis in the UK is therefore highly varied. Many are highly educated and professional – and thus could afford to bring their families away from the atrocities of war – but others are as a result of downward mobility either unemployed or in semi-skilled labour, despite being graduate professionals – a highly emotive subject.

There are several studies and reports that touch on Somalis' experience of settling in the UK, but some have had more attention than others. One area records the academic and social progress of Somali teenage boys, commenting on their 'unwelcome visibility' on the streets on the one hand and their introversion as a community on the other (Harris, 2004). The study by Sporton and Valentine (2007) focuses on the experience of Somali youth in the UK. Amidst much needed quantitative data, there are insights on subjects like identity, which shed light on some general attitudes. For example: 'Experiences of forced mobility and loss of attachment to place mean the identity "Muslim" becomes for many young Somali people the most important and consistent way that they have of defining who they are' (Sporton and Valentine, 2007: 1).

Research (Hussain, 2013; Harris, 2004) has also focused on mental health and Somali men, in whom there are particularly high rates of depression. Lone Somali mothers are also discussed, as there are women who came to the UK as widows after their husbands were killed in the war. Somali women have been prominent in representing their families in civic life in the UK and providing the backbone of their family's survival.

Not just 'other'

The mothers of Arab, mixed and English origin in my study were predominantly from the South East. All were working and of graduate level. Three of the mothers' children would be identified as 'mixed ethnicity' on census data. Living with two cultures brings with it unique challenges and benefits, which inform their narratives. The details about heritage and location are but a fraction of a more intricate portrait. Yet even this condensed look at ethnicity and migration highlights several differences that no doubt affect how mothers perceive their children's schooling and what they expect from it. I now consider how their views are heard and then shared.

Giving voice or hearing voice?

The concept of voice is problematic. Who can speak for whom? Where are they located? How is their position privileged? What are the power relations? The relationship between interviewer and interviewee is immensely complex. Within it, outside it, all around it lie critical views of what hearing, re-presenting and speaking for and about mean. Problematizing the act of hearing is inescapable out in the field. Whether I was arranging an interview, walking to the location, fine tuning the details of seating, timing or my own presentation, the question of who has a voice infused all considerations.

My research rests on the premise of giving marginalized women a voice in the discourse about parents and their children's education and the need to value their knowledge and experience. Elements of feminist research resonate with these aims – namely, looking at the participants' contexts and adopting a participatory method that is non-authoritarian and examines the knowledge generated in terms of the meanings the participants intend. Oakley's critical feminist approach to research sees subjectivity as a positive relationship between the researcher and the researched, as it yields richer, more honest narratives (Oakley, 1981).

Researcher positioning

My voice and role as the researcher raised some potential problems highlighted in the insider/outsider literature. Academics have written about the position of the 'insider' or 'outsider' researcher, exploring the dilemmas and considerations (amongst others, Mercer, 2007; Mirza, 1992; Mirza, 1998; Griffiths, 1998; Seale, 1999; Blaikie, 2000). These require reflection. Mirza, for example, explores her role as a black feminist researcher and the implications this has for her participants. Griffiths, meanwhile, questions the researcher's personal position and intention with regards to social justice. I found both approaches instructive.

The writings about 'autoethnography' (Ellis, 2003) also appealed to my experience, with the 'messiness and overlap' (2003: 215) of situating myself in the research. I readily identified with the notion of 'reflexive ethnography' – the considerable overlaps with faith and cultural background must have surely meant that my experiences affected the analysis of the data. It is in Kaye Haw's (1998) introspective position as a researcher, however, that I discovered an approach congruent with the theoretical stance of my research: '… a piece of research which does not give legitimacy to the "voice" of the researcher closes down the possibilities for critical dialogue and interaction'. My voice and role as a researcher in this small-scale study thus related to the insider/outsider discourse.

I had to restate my position and fine tune my relationships in every location I interviewed in. The more distant the participants were from my life, the less I needed to clarify my position. To them, I was a researcher whose credibility they didn't question; thy extended their trusting relationships with the gatekeeper to me. The gatekeepers were all Muslim women who worked in a school or organization that could provide access to mothers. In a similar vein the participants clearly approved that the research was an opportunity for the mothers to have their voices heard by educational professionals. The gatekeepers each processed the introductory information I sent them slightly differently. How they framed the research became apparent to me when participants expressed opinions asking me to tell 'them' that private school fees were too high, for example, as the quote at the beginning of this chapter shows. This suggested to me that participants had an exaggerated sense of my authority or agency in education. Other mothers wished me well with the research, saying that they hoped that teachers would benefit from knowing what *they* think and feel. I responded non-committedly. They saw me as sufficiently removed as an outsider to speak without caution or filters and, equally, as enough of an insider to be trusted to pick up on the cultural and faith-related nuances of their narratives.

The greatest challenge as an insider came from interviewing personal contacts. As Salmons (2015) observes, being an insider has the problems of belonging to the community in which the researcher and participants might share biases and 'the researcher is clearly in a position of power within the interview' (Salmons, 2015: 44). Having worked with adult learners for the past ten years, I have an insider understanding of the gender and family dynamics in their community. As an outsider, however, I lack experience of comprehensive secondary schools. Having experienced life as a minority student at selective schools only, both Church of England and Catholic, I did not want this aspect of my identity to surface in our discussions in case it increased the distance between our backgrounds.

Negotiating this role asked me to consider my 'multiple selves' (Birks and Mills, 2015: 18) from the outset. I therefore anticipated the conflicting and contradictory tensions of being at once an insider and outsider, and revisited them throughout the research and data analysis. I accepted that my insider self would make the analysis subjective to some degree, while my outsider self gave me a degree of distance from the participants. Reflexivity and my positionality permeate the rest of the book, as I discuss and interpret the data.

Research questions

A particular advantage of grounded theory is the way it does not confine the data to fit a particular concept. Instead, Glaser and Strauss – the founders of this approach – argue: 'Why not take the data and develop from them a theory that fits and works, instead of wasting time and good attempts to fit a theory based on 'reified' ideas of culture and social structure' (Glaser and Strauss, 1967: 262)?

In pursuit of grounded theory, I wanted the mothers' concerns to guide the subject matter of our conversation and their priorities to signpost the direction their narrative would go in. However, this approach risked allowing participants to dictate the contents of this book, which might have seen the data go off on a tangent that is unhelpful to educators. Alongside the grounded theory approach, I clearly required some parameters to shape their narratives.

I set the parameters to give coherence and depth for the reader and to ensure that the most pertinent issues were given due space. My parameters for ensuring the grounded approach were that:

- narratives must be relevant to education only, and not veer into areas of a participant's personal life, even though these relate to their child's wellbeing and education in the broader sense
- their curriculum-related and non-academic related interactions were equally important in understanding their relationship with the school and teachers
- any confidential cases involving Social Services should not be discussed
- we are exploring school-related matters and not personality clashes with members of staff.

The research questions were divided into two areas: mothers' own definitions and ideas about what education meant and still means to them, bound within their own identity, and the public sphere of interacting with the school system.

The first question was about their **identity**, to contextualize the research. I had called the project 'Muslim mothers', although I was well aware of the pitfalls of homogenization facing any group of people given a single label. In public discourse over the past two decades, however, the term Muslim has increasingly become a simplistic label, hiding the individuality, breadth and diversity of over 3 million people in the UK.

Challenging the entire faith identity was beyond the scope of my small-scale study, hence the project was presented as 'Muslim Mothers' without deconstructing how the label came into being. What I did ask, however, was whether this was a way that the mothers would identify themselves?

Accordingly, I asked them about their own framework for what education meant for them, and for their children. I wished to elicit their own definitions of how they perceive education, what it encompasses, what has influenced their vision and whether and how it differs from their own experience of education. This question also accommodated the participants' breadth of culture and how they understood the word 'education' in different ways depending on the cultural factors at play.

Moving on from the inner realm of their identity and perceptions of education, came the questions for the outer realm: how did they go about choosing their children's schools/nurseries/early years education? What influenced their decisions? The next category of questions probed their experience more specifically:

- how have you found your interaction/ communication with the school?
- do you find anything challenging?
- are there any examples of communications that went well?

The final group of questions invited participants to address practitioners directly, as though they were talking to them and could convey one or two key messages that would help them in their relationships with Muslim children – particularly theirs – and their parents.

Analysing the data was an ongoing process, particularly as the interviews and focus groups were staggered. Some individuals in each focus group were interviewed again on their own, which allowed me to probe themes they brought up themselves. This method, aligned to 'responsive-interviewing' (Rubin and Rubin, 2012), allowed for a deeper understanding of what participants wanted to convey. The transcripts of the interviews were analysed for recurring themes and phrases and the ways the mothers constructed their personal narratives elaborating on public debates. I said as little as possible in the individual interviews, allowing the 'free-association' to produce a multitude of themes about education and their lives. Many of these were too disparate to discuss fully. I then combed both the transcripts and my personal journal-style notes, which I wrote straight after each interview and immediately after the focus groups, purely to harness the unspoken: the body language, hesitations, questions and – almost always – the important opinions expressed after the interview was formally ended. I also compared recordings and notes of the individual mothers to the data from the community they were familiar with.

Maintaining the thread of reflexivity throughout the research process, I was aware of the fact that what I was seeking to share would be affected by the interaction the mothers had with me. Pezella *et al.*'s (2012) illuminating demonstration of the rapport between participant and researcher showed how three researchers asking their teenage sample exactly the same questions amassed vastly different data. Her analysis of the interviewers' personalities resulted in three typologies – 'neutral', 'interpretive' and 'affirmative' – that drew out different responses. I was troubled by the reality that another group of mothers with another researcher might elicit a whole new set of narratives and themes. Should these dilemmas be reason not to conduct the research? Would it be better to leave the shadows in the margins? Could educators who need to communicate with Muslim mothers find their own way, unique to their own circumstance and therefore more authentic? Instead of abandoning the process under the weight of these questions,

I accepted that some voices, with all the imperfections that surround the mechanics of sharing them, are better than the void.

A combination of limited time and resources, and the similar answers I received in the individual interviews, drew a line under the process. After the initial interviews and focus groups were conducted, only four more participants were invited, in an attempt to widen the breadth of ethnic backgrounds. In Chapter 4 I present the data on the overarching themes of identity, how education is viewed and the mothers' choice of school.

Chapter 4

Identities, education and school choice

I'm a working mum. That's how I see myself… a working mum.

(Asiyah)

I don't want to be a stereotype reactionary Muslim mother.

(Saba)

I also didn't want a school where there was cultural confusion with a Muslim identity. So the fewer the Muslims, in one way the better.

(Nasra)

I wanted a good education to help them to have a good career in the future – that's my main priority.

(Husna)

Education … it's not just doing English and maths, it's about your spiritual side as well.

(Hibaaq)

This chapter is the first of four dominated by the data from my empirical research. It explores three of the 'macro' or overarching questions: about the mothers' identities, their views on what 'education' means to them and how mothers in this study made school choices. The emphasis is entirely down to how they interpreted the question and in the case of the focus groups, how the question was passed between participants to collectively shape their answer.

The excerpts illustrate both popular responses as well as instances where a few mothers interpreted the subject matter in a different way to the others. The combination of dual methods – individual interviews and two focus groups – led the same question to be discussed in different ways. As one would expect, the individual interviews provided more depth, whilst generally, the focus groups provided breadth as participants responded to each other. Together, as a montage, they each add their own shape, texture and depth to situate themselves, building their own narrative.

The exploratory questions I asked were:

- this project is called 'Muslim mothers and their children's school'. How would you identify yourself? Would you use anything (nationality, country, faith, job title) before Mum, just Mum or something else?
- what does 'education' mean to you? What does it include?
- how did you make the choice of school for your children?

Identity

As I've discussed, identity as a concept can be understood in different ways. For the mothers in my study, the subject was raised in the context of the project's working title: 'Muslim mothers and their children's schools.' Was this a relevant, honest title for them? Would they wish to change it? These were the type of discussion starters I used.

The responses I got back showed the way the mothers identified themselves and the way they felt they were identified in the school context. For many, 'identity' was a journey, hence they needed to travel through their own turns and pauses along the way.

> I'm a Muslim and a mum. It's a different world. It's a responsibility of not just raising children but raising them in a certain way ... so we have a lot more expectations on ourselves for this life and the next. So I guess it's not just looking after them, it's certain values and morals ...
>
> (Nilofer, teacher, L5)

> I am obviously a Muslim, from my outer appearance that's already obvious when they see me and the identity I'm giving my child is Muslim as the cultural one can be a bit confusing. The way I'm raising her is Islam inspired, so yes, a Muslim mother identity is what I'd use for the state sector. Maybe it's because of the culture I grew up with. Growing up, up north in the 90s, there was no Arab culture there, and we were often called 'Paki' – as the Asian box was all we fitted in to, or were seen to fit in to.
>
> (Nasra, teacher, L5)

* * *

I'm a Muslim woman and a Somali mother so my main identity is a Muslim woman/mother. This covers everything – my religion is a way of life, so, if I want to be a good citizen, mother, woman, I have to be a good Muslim ... that's what I think. That's my identity. I'm trying to raise my children to be Muslim girls. That's the most important.

(Hibaaq, homemaker, L3)

We have to show who we are because of the wrong ideas. We can do everything, say everything. We are Muslim, we respect other religions ...

(Hodan, homemaker, L3)

Yes, like the media ... all this propaganda, especially about women. I feel very proud as a mother.

(Amaal, care assistant, L3)

These mothers are explicit about their faith being a way of life that affects how they raise their children, including the belief in accountability, as Nilofer alluded to when she includes 'the next' life – the belief in an afterlife – as an implicit part of her identity. Similar to most of the women in my study, these mothers immediately linked how they see themselves to the conscious identity they wanted for their children. The second quotation makes an important distinction between faith and culture, the former preferred over the latter – particularly because this mother experienced cross-cultural racism in her youth and for her culture carries a negative association. Homogenizing minority identities is not new, particularly if we consider experiences through a racialized lens. What is interesting, however, is how clearly we can see how it influences choices made two, or three decades later. The short exchange during the focus group meeting in location 3 adds another dimension to these mothers' similarly decisive and forthright identities. Here, Hodan and Amaal decide they must assert agency and resist the media stereotype of being uneducated and oppressed. Amaal, as we see in Chapter 7, has good reason to 'feel proud'.

Time and location

Their location, and how this affected them, was a significant subject for approximately a third of mothers. The quote below shows how for this particular participant, simply being a mother was foremost in her mind. It also shows how her 'mother' identity was received. Ethnicity is brushed aside as unimportant in this context, where details, though unspoken

– such as how many children a woman has and the nuances around age and motherhood – are part of the subtext. Time and location are raised by Asiyah, whose children are older. She divides her identity between her physical daily reality and her spiritual being:

> I'd say I'm a mother of four ... people can already see me with my scarf, so I never have to identify myself. Everyone's so integrated it doesn't matter if you're Pakistani, Bangladeshi or Indian, so to me the important thing is I'm a mum of four. I get quite a shocked reaction, as it's considered a lot ... like having four. Sometimes I avoid the whole 'mother' thing because people I work with don't believe I've got teenage kids ... I don't know what their assumptions are, but they'll say I don't look like I've got children and all that. So, sometimes I just want to get the whole mother thing out of the way, and say ... ok I'm a mother of four. That's it.
>
> (Saba, counsellor, L5)

> I'd call myself a working mother. Then I'd have the faith identity.
>
> (Asiyah, corporate manager, L5)

> Identity ... umm ... it depends on where you are. When Rema was at (type B) school, with more Asians, I was just another parent. They did all the halal whatever, you don't have to bother. But at (type A) school – it's less mixed – you have to make a point. Like there's things I don't do: like sleepovers, discos ... I don't know what secondary school's like because I've got just primary. It's about finding a balance between private and public identities. My child's the only Asian in the class. We're consciously giving her a Muslim identity. She's a British person. They only get the Asian bit through food, a tiny bit of language (even the few words they know are Anglicized), so you've got to have something ... you know, something. There isn't much culture left, so they've got religion.
>
> (Parveen, learning support assistant, L5)

Parveen's thinking about her identity is attached to both place and ethnic make-up, and to some extent the age of her children. She mentions that not having to do anything because the school was already aware of dietary needs due to the large intake of Asian children (implying Muslim children), has the effect of anonymizing her in terms of faith – it doesn't need identifying. However, in the less diverse school faith becomes prioritized when Parveen needs to fulfil her responsibilities. As other studies have found, for second generation British Bangladeshi-born parents, the link with heritage becomes weaker.

The personal journey

Some mothers explored the concept of identity in greater depth, focusing on their personal journeys, the influences and changes, which were embedded in the overarching framework of their children's education. Their reflexive accounts raise disparate themes as they question when and why changes to their identity came about. Since their extracts about identity show a process of reflection, I present them in their entirety.

> Zainab: I definitely see myself as a Muslim mother. But it has gradually grown. I always thought of myself as just a 'mum' not as a Muslim mum. But when I came here, spent some years here, that's when I thought I should be known as a Muslim mother, not just a mother. What shall I say … it's more … more powerful I think. Where I came from was all mixed in India. Christian, Hindu, Muslim, we lived in unity, we lived like a family, it was amazing. We were in and out of our neighbours' house, they were in our house, schools were all mixed … it was so much fun. We went to each other's festivals, it wasn't any [big] thing to do that.
>
> SD: So it was very mixed, back in India?
>
> Z: Yes, we went to each other's celebrations. That was until I came here in '97. After 9/11, that's when everyone started bringing that identity to us. You know 'Muslim this, Muslim that', 'British Muslim' … I think after that, yeah … definitely, I never thought about that before … I have to be honest.
>
> SD: Who do you mean was 'bringing that identity'?
>
> Z: Mainly the media, of course. The media was giving this message – then gradually that was getting into each and every community, that there is a 'Muslim this' and a 'Muslim that'. What I found out was that even Indians stopped recognizing us as Indian, we were Muslim. So I found out we are a community of Muslims, we don't have a nationality.
>
> SD: Which nationality do you mean?
>
> Z: I want to identify as Indian, I do. But that generalization came gradually. Like through school. People made assumptions that if

you're Muslim you must be Pakistani. People don't even know there are Muslims in India! In the beginning the school made the assumption that we weren't interested in our children's education and things like that. But I wanted to make sure and change that. I'm completely interested in my kid's education and I wanted the teachers to know. I wanted them to know I'm interested in my daughter's education and I was involved from day one.

(Zainab, medical health professional, L5)

* * *

Asma: I would say, I'm a mother, integrated in this society. To communicate with everyone around me, I'd say, I am a mum, just a mum. But personally to clarify things, I'm a Muslim mum. When people see me, they think 'that's a Muslim mum' anyway, but that's just appearance. For me, I'd like to be known as a Muslim mum now … but that's changed, from, say 10 years ago.

SD: Why's that?

A: Because I feel a need to be clearer … two … it's two things. It's people's perception and it's from me; who I am. Before I wasn't fussed about it, I was just a mum. I think as I've got older, the need to be clearer in my own life … if I'm being clear or not … the need to have that for my children …

SD: What do you mean by 'being clearer'?

A: I think it's partly to do with doing *Umrah*, yes, going on *Umrah*. Partly to do with age, confidence, thought process to say 'actually I'm happy with this', it's partly exercising my choice and my personal journey, yeah, confidence, I'd say has a lot to do with it.

(Asma, learning support assistant, L5)

* * *

Bushra: Before my kids went to school, I'd just say 'I'm a mum'. I wouldn't add Pakistani, or think of anything like that. I saw myself as just a mum. But when I started to go to schools, then I was forced to be a 'Muslim mother'.

SD: Why was that?

B: Because people see you differently. There's a judgement made ... in terms of acceptance, there isn't that automatic friendship that you'd strike up with a mum irrespective of their background, like setting up play-dates. It's automatically imposed, it becomes an issue.

SD: What do you mean by 'an issue'?

B: I think naturally people are inclined towards people like them, I expected that. Like it's clearly easy for my child to go to another Muslim child's house ... in terms of food and things, but I didn't expect that much difference with other mothers. ... I expected some cultural differences ... I have questioned if I'm paranoid, like just asking for a play date, or just talking in the playground, the 'Muslim' badge sticks out. But it's like non-Muslim parents are ... it's like they're star struck. And I think it's coming from the media – that plays a big part in it. People are really influenced by the media.

(Bushra, student, L5)

Any discussion about identity will reveal its evolving nature, its fluidity and transmutability. These mothers touched on this by retracing how, in Zainab's words, a variety of factors – migration, ethnicity, inter-faith, global events and the media – all merge into what is described as a replacement of cultural identity with a faith identity. Zainab shows how she prioritizes faith in her children's upbringing and education. However, at the juncture of identity, the sense of an imposition – of having the faith label imposed from a place of negativity – comes across. Asma, in contrast, has evolved through her own spiritual journey, attributed to pilgrimage, and she equates the 'Muslim mother' identity with growing in confidence and choosing to wear this label. Like several others in this study, she has also highlighted the fact wearing the hijab already identifies her as a Muslim in the eyes of the school – hence the exploration on a more personal level.

The following – and final – extract from Wahida highlights the way she internalized public opinion. Wahida raised her identity as a mother at the start. Two things come out of her response: first, the mismatch between her expectations of how she would like her school relationships to be and second, how this disjunct is, in her view, caused by global events that make it into the playground and differentiate her, contrary to her desire to fit in, make friends and not be viewed differently. There are similarities to the way Hodan asserts the need to challenge the deficit model of the oppressed Muslim woman earlier in this chapter:

Wahida: I think it depends on the different scenarios, because being Muslim is such a part of me, I don't stop to think about it – a huge part of me is being Muslim. But in terms of being a mother – I'm driven by other things …

SD: What drives you?

W: Cultural influence, and the places I've lived in, London, being part of diverse British society with people from different backgrounds. The fact that I'm born and raised here and have parent's culture and faith – the faith moulds a big part.

(Wahida, medical health professional, L5)

* * *

In location 4, putting 'Muslim' before 'mum' sparked debate as a label the women received because of their appearance, despite not being conscious of it on a daily basis. Tahira was emphatic about it being an unnatural way to think about themselves, and compared it to other mothers with a faith, who she believed *'wouldn't go round thinking, "I'm a Christian Mum", or "I'm a Jewish Mum"'*. The debate continued:

T: I see myself as a mother of Muslim children. When I'm at school I'm a mum. As a governor, I wasn't there for Muslim children, I was there for everyone. I am a parent – my children are Muslim, so they have certain needs, or concerns, but I don't go around thinking about 'being' a Muslim mother, I'm a mum.

(Tahira, educationalist/activist, L4)

A: I think the reason why I'd say Muslim mother, is because there are a lot of things that differentiate … maybe 'cos mine are all at school (primary and secondary) at the moment; PE, clothes, food etc. – there are quite a few things I deal with – but that doesn't mean I don't participate and care about other things as well. For instance, when they do academic stuff, as a mother I'm involved. It's a bit of both, being a mum.

(Amira, solicitor, L4)

M: Now that Tahira has said that, I just see myself as a parent as well, not a 'Muslim mother'.

(Mariam, school admin, L4)

H: But maybe it depends on what they're doing. 'Cos we're the parents, it's for us to teach them. So it depends what's happening. Like my son asked about a disco. I said we are Muslim we don't go disco. I says 'do you see your mum and dad go disco? Do you know what it is? Do you like flashing lights and loud music?' So we have to teach them ... and then that's the type of mother we are.

(Huda, part-time student/ homemaker, L4)

This group discussion evolved into a self-critical exercise, looking at different sections within the 'Muslim' community, which is of relevance to the next chapter. In the follow-up individual interview, Tahira referred to the 'work' she puts in as a parent to be seen by the school in a particular way. The complexities about identity unravelled thus:

It's that need to show, I am just a parent and that we're not all the same, and perhaps undo some of the stereotypes. And ... if I wasn't wearing this scarf, if I wasn't identified as Muslim, I wonder if the attitude of the teachers would be different and then I wouldn't have to work so hard.

Other mothers spoke about the effort that goes into projecting an identity that differentiates them from stereotypes about Muslims parents. When Saba says, 'I don't want to be a stereotype reactionary Muslim mother,' she echoes the group identity of the Muslim parents Tahira was alluding to. Issues of intra-ethnic class, education level and religiosity intersect here, differentiating mothers from different backgrounds. Tahira and Saba want to distance themselves from the stereotypical 'reactionary': the demanding mother who appears at school to complain and is seen as a nuisance. This theme is revisited by several mothers in ensuing chapters, who repeatedly express their need to clarify exactly what 'type' of Muslim mother they are.

And ... 'this'

The interview questions did not include any references to clothes or appearance. In the course of discussing their identity, however, mothers made passing comments about how they felt they were seen in relation to how they looked. 'I'm a Muslim mum, and well they see this don't they' – a comment accompanied by a point or tug at their hijab. Although it wasn't addressed explicitly, the hijab – a scarf covering the hair – was gestured to by several mothers in the individual interviews. Out of the 51 mothers, only seven did not wear hijab. None of them wore the face veil (niqab), which has occupied a disproportional amount of space in public discourse on Muslim women. As I was also wearing the hijab, there was a tacit understanding that they didn't need to expand on what effect it has when one wears it. Nonetheless, identity discussions expanded along such lines – participants mentioned inviting assumptions of being uneducated or being seen as potentially unwelcome in school. One mother described at length awaiting an appeal date for a secondary school place for her daughter, and her preparation for the appeal panel interview, concluding: 'I don't want people to judge me. When I walk in, I'm going in as a mother, representing my child, but maybe "this" (touching her scarf) could go against me, I don't know' (Sonia, admin, L1).

Collectively, what came across, apart from an affirmation of how they saw themselves, was the need for those mothers with higher education qualifications to distinguish themselves from those without. Two mothers who did not wear the hijab, had little to say about how they were seen. Their silence on the theme of identity reflected their priority during their interviews to 'blend in' and 'not stand out', as one of them – Emma (medical health professional, L5) – clearly stated.

When discussing identity, women spoke about how their personas were re-evaluated by their colleagues when they started to wear the hijab. One senior manager in a school found:

> I was asked questions like: 'Did your husband make you wear it?' How could they think that … they knew me but they still asked something like this. I had to explain it was my own decision, which it was. I wanted to wear it, and it's made me more conscious of who I am. But I did get a lot of comments … like how I looked before.
>
> (Afreen, deputy headteacher, L5)

My own experiences made me firmly an 'insider' on this topic, as I had encountered various assumptions over the years. While varying waves of confusion about the reason for wearing the hijab have come and gone in the past two decades, the common denominator has been the disbelief that a woman born and educated in the West can make the personal spiritual choice to adopt the hijab (Afshar, 2008). If the hijab is rationalized, as I find, it is interpreted as a statement of political resistance; again contrary to real, lived experiences. Countless discussions with Muslim women about faith and spirituality constitute personal testimony to the fact that for those who choose to dress this way, it is not necessarily a political statement but comes from the intangible – faith. In the grand scheme of belief and practice, the hijab is a minor part of faith, which due to its visibility has become a symbol on which to hang ever more intriguing misconceptions. Identities proved to be an emotive subject, a messy combination of the women projecting, defending and creating themselves as mothers – a process which in itself is challenging to women. The following data on what education means to the mothers, afforded another opportunity to explain their point of view on this pivotal subject.

What does education mean to you?

Participants interpreted this question largely in practical terms, with some offering philosophical input. Their answers ventured back into the territory of their own education and what bearing this had had on their present definitions.

Holistic views of education

A common response from those who chose to elaborate on the subject was that 'education' encompassed a child's whole upbringing: morals, values, citizenship, faith as well as traditional academic subjects. Individual interviews and focus group data from participants of different ethnicities and socio-economic backgrounds produced succinct definitions of what education means to them:

> I always wanted both academic and Islamic education to be equal as well ... I used to do additional literacy and numeracy every day. I used to encourage them to do all the clubs, all extracurricular in primary and secondary, encouraged them to join the extracurricular activities at school.
>
> (Zainab)

> Education is the base of living ... of everything. It's not just English and maths, it's about your spiritual side as well.
>
> (Hibaaq)

> If you are educated you can challenge and talk ... you can debate, with complete knowledge ... you know your rights, you know the law, you can defend yourself, as a mother if you don't know your rights, people become aggressive. If you can't express, and you don't know your rights, you become frustrated and angry. It's very important to get a solid education. I emphasize you have to be educated otherwise you are insecure. You have to have education of both things.
>
> (Hodan)

I'd say a sound education is one where my daughters are pushed, challenged and supported. Their experiences should be wide, with opportunities and a chance of good integration.

> (Rizwana, learning support assistant, L3)

I never appreciated how much time I'd have to put in – [because of] the impact of the class size. I expected it to be more holistic, like generic moral values, the whole of a child … it was more bitty than I expected.

> (Jameela, postgraduate researcher/teacher, L5)

***

Focus group in location 2

B: Education and values are important. We just want the best for our children, education is about passing on *salah* (daily prayers) and the other subjects.

A: And respect is another part of education, and manners.

F: Academic is very important as part of education.

A: The problem is with the parents who don't know how to read and write, they'll struggle to help with education. My parents did push, and I learnt to read and write. But I couldn't get help from them, back in the day, in the 1970s.

I: Education is necessary for their future, for the country. General education in school isn't enough. What's important with this is that they go to mosque, in their environment, with people, and learn manners and how to behave appropriately. And learning Bangla. It's not just books and pens … it's manners, respect – it's all education.

B: We live in a multi culture, so they need to learn about living with everyone in the community. They have to mix with everyone.

The mothers in the focus group also saw civic responsibility, faith, academic achievement and knowing how to navigate personal relations as part of education. Their view of education as all-encompassing is exemplified in the popular concept of *tarbiyah* – see Chapter 3. Similarly, mothers across all locations mentioned upbringing, with five adding 'extra-curricular activities, sports and music facilities' as part of education. In *Nurturing Muslim*

Childhood, which focuses on how Muslim families raise their children, Scourfield *et al.* (2013) make a similar connection about upbringing and imparting religious education. It is also found in the families at the centre of their research, who 'demonstrate the mutual obligations of parents and children towards one another, including the parental responsibility for the religious nurture and education of children' (Scourfield *et al.*, 2013: 22).

The more recent migrants (L2 and L3) noted the personal safety aspect of being 'educated', emphasizing 'rights' and not getting frustrated when interacting with people. This was a common issue for such parents, who were struggling with language acquisition, being in a new home and dealing with a new education system (Open Society, 2014).

On school choice

A huge subject in its own right, school choice was either pursued in depth or skipped over as of no interest. Typically, the mothers who had either high levels of education or established careers had more to say on the subject. Individual interviews permitted extended narratives, some of which lasted the whole interview and centred on this particular subject. Factors such as having more than two children made some narratives longer than others, as mothers shared a variety of experiences. Those who made a conscious decision about school choice described adopting similar techniques when choosing both primary and secondary schools. These included: looking at Ofsted reports, asking friends about Ofsted ratings and finding out from their social networks – 'I heard it on the grapevine' (Ball and Vincent, 1998). Distance and transport were limiting factors, especially for non-drivers.

Local and convenient

For the focus group mothers, particularly those with children in the council estate schools, close proximity and diversity were the main priorities. The UK-born mothers, particularly those from location 2, stressed high standards, 'good management', it being 'easy to communicate with the teachers' and 'distance from home'. Those who found it difficult to understand the education system relied heavily on information from neighbours and other parents:

> My two sisters-in-law worked in a school and they advised me. My husband went to the same primary school, there was a Bengali interpreter there too. At first I was scared when they started school and then I realized they [staff] help you.
>
> (Shama, volunteer nursery assistant, L1)

Many mothers echoed these sentiments:

> My expectation was good company – to have good company –
> you choose a school with a good catchment area, well-educated
> people, that's how you get a good school. We looked at Ofsted
> reports, we had liked a church school, because it had more
> discipline, like you hear faith schools are better.
>
> (Dina, mosque teacher/ learning support assistant, L5)

Looking for 'a feeling', feeling like 'fitting in'

Mothers who were aware of the convergence of race, faith, public opinion
and global events on the school site made their choices strategically. A few
– less than a fifth – spoke about moving house to be in a location that had
the 'mix' of what they were looking for:

> Wahida: We were looking for the moral feel, discipline,
> academics. Even though we were in the catchment for a good
> school, we ended up in a Christian private school – C of E – we
> liked a small school, and the moral feel to start off with but not
> affordable long term. We did a lot of visiting schools. We trusted
> the Montessori head and she was a good source of information
> as well. In [county name] we have the state schools, but not good
> local options, I visited so many before we moved, C of E, in small
> villages and all sorts of places. We were coming from a diverse
> part of London. Going local we'd blend in, but we weren't happy
> about what we were reading – like the academic side and general
> behaviour report, leadership, management … and hearsay as
> well. But if we looked out, a bit further, it was one culture. Now,
> I'd make more of an effort to look locally. We weren't happy we
> had to travel further to a better school than a poorer local school.

> SD: Why was that?

> W: I was meeting the head and it was very obvious … we went
> to a top league-table school, but the minute the head saw me he
> went bright red, a physical reaction he couldn't hide … made me
> uncomfortable, even though he was very nice … I felt he was a
> bit tense. I decided no. Crossed it off. He wasn't as relaxed as
> other heads who didn't bat an eyelid when they met me. Like the
> current school, I was comfortable with the head.

To be honest, in those days, I made a point of wearing colourful scarves and keeping away from too much black, maybe my own prejudice, and guessing how they may think when they see me. It's a subconscious thing, I went for colours when I went to see a school.

SD: So appearance mattered?

W: Well … I was trying to suss out a place where my children would feel at home. In one of the first schools – a headteacher was cold and unwelcoming – and I'd rather drive further to a school where the head was warmer and more welcoming. I thought if I don't feel comfortable, how would my children be? Children are children, they just have a natural need to belong, have friends, blend in, feel comfortable. They won't want to feel like they're weird.

(Wahida)

* * *

First primary school when we moved wasn't that good, but it was the only one with a place, so as it wasn't doing well I moved them to a better school. It wasn't academic enough, the families lacked aspiration, not what I was looking for, and there was no ethnic mix – we were the only Muslim family. For me, the main thing is aspiration, what do the parents want for their children, that's what matters.

(Saba)

* * *

My parents' expectations were the same as when they were in the Middle East, trusting the system, thinking that there was no need to select, just go to the nearest school. When we reached secondary, then they realized that not all schools were the same or the type of people in them. We moved down south and I started my A-levels in a school with lots of Arabs. That's where I saw disadvantages to being with a lot of Muslim girls as cultural and family practices that were different to my family were part of the way they were and that led to confusion, if it wasn't for my parents' firm hold on what they thought was right and not right.

Because of these experiences, I chose my daughter's school on two different concerns: 1. The nursery teaching styles when she was nursery age – I liked the Montessori method – and that had an impact on her, that I wanted to find in the primary school she was going to go on to. 2. I wanted a school where there wasn't too many children for whom EAL, and then resources would go to those children. I also didn't want a school where there was culture confused with a Muslim identity. So the fewer the Muslims, in one way the better.

(Nasra)

***

For primary, on our first visit we found the setting was really nice, semi-countryside, children looked happy yet it was disciplined, children looked like they were enjoying what they were doing. But I didn't quite get a warm feel from the head – I was neutral. Nothing worried me. I liked the school and staff a lot. Despite it being not ethnically mixed at all, I preferred that.

There was an ethnically mixed school near us but that had kids with bad manners in the playground and that put me off. In the end she went to the further one, and we had new neighbours who spoke highly of the school – one who was Indian. But I had reservations as it was less ethnically mixed, and I knew I had to get involved.

(Jameela)

***

There's a cultural aspect to the religion, like Egyptian culture isn't the same as Pakistani. So I didn't want them in a heavily Asian school, as they wouldn't fit in again. We live in this country and we need the children to fit in here in this country. I feel my children need to learn about other religions, and get on with everyone with different cultures and ways of life. That's important to me … because we see that it's up to parents to guide them. Because also, my family is English as well, so they've got that too. They've got to respect that too, they need to know where they fit in.

(Emma)

Nasra, Jameela and Emma articulated the responses common to the mothers from similar socio-economic and educational backgrounds: their selection of schools was a deliberate process, involving moving house, carefully checking a school's ethnic make-up and prioritizing manners and behaviour. They also wanted the 'feeling' of being accepted by the staff. The similarity in several mothers' accounts about how headteachers and staff responded to them highlights the delicate ways they test the water for their children. Because Nasra, Jameela and Emma have different ethnic backgrounds, their faith identity becomes crucial: would my child, would we, be accepted here as a Muslim family? Wahida was particularly explicit, describing her concerted effort to wear colourful head scarves so as not to come across as a stereotype – implying her wish to avoid presenting a negative image of a Muslim woman. Her need for warmth and acceptance reveals her multi-layered consideration in the search for a school where her child's ethnicity and faith can sit comfortably alongside the aforementioned standards for academic achievement and behaviour.

Mothers of the same socio-economic and educational background shared a narrative of school choice that clearly differentiated culture from faith, and avoided the influence on their children of any one ethnic group. Such issues of class are nothing new. Louise Archer (2010) for example, looked at how ethnic minority parents managed their children's school careers. Respondents in her study, who came from a range of ethnic minority backgrounds, explained their struggles with the education system to make sure their children progressed. They utilized their middle-class capital to avert the effects of low expectations and in some cases stereotyping. There are classed choices apparent in the aforementioned quotes, echoing the data from location 4's focus group, who don't want to be thought of as being like 'those Muslims'.

Educational standards were at times conflated with ethnic considerations. Searching for schools with fewer children with EAL in a class is one example of the belief that being among children from the dominant culture would benefit their child's language development. A professional mother from location 1 saw things differently, regarding the fact that 99 per cent of her first child's school was from an ethnic minority as 'wonderful because of the strong leadership' (Rehana, officer, L1).

Going the extra mile

Apart from the focus group mothers in location 3, there were a few who made additional efforts in their search, application and knowledge of the system. The mothers in location 3 scarcely mentioned choice of primary school because they had a school on the housing estate where they all lived – it was an automatic choice. Their response is in keeping with several studies of working-class minority parents in the UK and their experiences of sending their children to the nearest school.

However, some mothers in the study from every part of the socio-economic spectrum made every effort to go further afield if they thought it would help their children achieve academically and morally. These aspirational women, whatever their economic status or educational background, spoke of the detailed studies they made of the schools they were considering – the location in terms of the neighbourhoods reputation, the 'type' of children already there, the higher education destinations of past students – and all were adamant that it was their responsibility as a mother to make an informed choice:

> Husna: I look for the best schooling, Ofsted report, family friends … I look into my schools. If it means I have to travel out, I will. Husband's more into safety and near. I'm not like that. I think they should be thrown in, and not just Asian community, and not many friends, it'll balance out. First, I was living with in laws, and my daughter went to where was near. As soon as I moved out, I looked around, I chose the good ones and went through appeal and she got in.
>
> SD: How do you define a good school?
>
> H: How long teachers stay in a school and stick it out, not keen on teachers moving a lot. If they're there for long, that shows a good sign. Also with that Ofsted report – outstanding, good … and all that. Yes there are other schools doing well. But I live in an area of deprivation, and there's more supply teachers coming in.
>
> (Husna, project officer, L1)

In Phillips's (2009) research on the way young British Muslim women create and negotiate their home spaces, data from participants in the North of England spoke of the entwined expectations of family ties, negotiating where they lived and managing their degrees of autonomy. As Husna says, whether or not you live with in-laws becomes a factor in school choice. Asserting parental choice therefore involves more than the distance to the school, Ofsted inspection results and available spaces. There are areas of home life to evaluate and manage, so the family home set-up becomes important. In line with Sonia's comments regarding school catchment areas about crossing ethnic boundaries, women in Phillips's study described their calculated choice to move away from their own community. This was not without careful consideration, however, as Phillips illuminates here:

> More young British Muslims are moving into new spaces, although there are perceived risks attached. Women raised worries about racist harassment, racism, feeling 'out of place' and their capacity to fulfil their duty to transmit an Islamic identity on to their children if they lived in a 'white' area. Neighbourhoods beyond the ethnic community areas may thus be viewed as potential sites of anxiety, especially for veiled Muslim women, as compared with the relative predictability and security of inner areas.
>
> (Phillips, 2009: 33)

Regarding secondary school choice for an older daughter, one participant outlined her criteria thus:

> I looked all over, my daughter got a good school in catchment but I declined because I heard there were some gangs even though education was outstanding. I heard girls go in and they change their identity. It's a crucial year, when they go in they can change and I want them to be strong. We live in an area with a lot of Asians and Asian culture – it's not Islam. I had to move her away from that. Where she went here was only two girls with hijab. She integrated really well … they were all white British in YR 8. I felt it was ok, she mixed in well. I feel she's more confident and vocal …
>
> I don't mind a mixed school, they'll be working one day, and I think they need to know how to work. I think it's good to integrate in our society … to live your life to build something in your life and you have to deal with both genders. University is mixed. I wanted my daughter to make sure she gets on with different backgrounds and appreciate her own as well. There's gonna be social issues … she's got good friends with a mixture, the majority are English, one Somali. I didn't make her wear hijab, and she got in there with it.
>
> (Husna)

For secondary choice, it's led by my daughter who's keen. But I must say we're keen on a girls' school to deal with all those issues … like boyfriends and all that. I've been hearing what people have to deal with and I'm worried.

I'm basing our choice on my daughter's ability, emotion, needs. And then, a single-sex school, I presume I'd be dealing with all the other things too, so I'd rather take this easier option.

(Emma)

These comments show such mothers using 'aspirational capitals' (Basit, 2012) and to some extent 'emotional capitals' (Reay, 2000; Gillies, 2006) to support the best education they can for their children. Basit's study of minority youth provides ample evidence that families have a pivotal role in raising young people's chances of social mobility and high attainment. Like other mothers with the same drive, they use the resources available to them – often without the cultural capitals – to navigate the best outcome. Husna mentioned the long-term destination of higher education and careers when thinking about school choice.

The age range of the participants' children was another factor affecting choice of school. They discussed choice of secondary school far less than of primary school. When they did, single-sex schools were not their foremost priority, contrary to the essentialized view that all Muslim parents wish for single-sex schools. The preference for single-sex schools, can, as Ijaz and Abbas' (2010) empirical evidence endorses, be related to which community and generation are expressing their views. The authors compared inter-generational Mirpuri parents' views on educating daughters and found that while the majority were positive about their education, there were differences in purpose. Older parents saw mixed schools as promoting free mixing and a devaluation of marriage, whereas younger parents viewed education as empowerment and put greater emphasis on their faith and assimilation into society. Correspondingly, the younger mothers in my study, who were all from diverse backgrounds, felt that ethnic mix, the type of company and the elusive criterion of fitting-in were of more importance than the issue of single-sex verses mixed schools.

Data from mothers in less affluent areas showed that such mothers knew where the better schools were but were out of their catchment areas and consequently hard to get to. Location has always played a key role in school choice (Ball and Vincent, 1998; Burgess, 2009; Exely, 2011). Whereabouts in England participants lived also influenced how secondary school places were allocated. Location 5, for example, has a two-tier system, with both selective grammars – state-funded secondary schools that require pupils to pass an exam (the 11+) aged 11 to gain entry – and non-selective schools. Here the subject of school choice is further complicated by arguments for or against selection. None of the mothers entered this debate, but they did mention the options they had thought about if their children didn't pass the selection exams.

From these three broad areas – their identity as mothers, how they define education and the way they make their school choices – one can see how, to different degrees, the mothers' sense of responsibility for their children's spiritual development intertwines with their interest in academic attainment. The strength of their opinions is evident in their long-term, considered thoughts, the criticality they showed when making their choices and the decision to change direction when they felt the schools their children were going to did not meet their expectations. At the heart of the mothers' narratives was their sensitivity to their identity being accepted, and the way they wanted to be positioned through that identity. In Chapter 5 I cast light on specific areas of the interactions between the mothers and the schools. I also look at the variety of ways of communicating – from formal invitations to the unspoken laws of the playground – and the way relationships are formed, and not formed. Lastly I offer insights into some of the most commonly discussed dilemmas of parent–school rapport.

Relationships
From playground pariah to inclusion governor

You have to be really special to be accepted, you know, really exceptional, like Mo Farah or something.

(Saba)

Every summer fair I volunteer, I've gone in to help with activities. I've tried to be part of the school community and I think it went really well.

(Jameela)

You see that everything that is news-based plays out in the playground.

(Bushra)

They know what a church is, a synagogue is ... that's all fine they do them in religious lessons. They've been to them too, a church and synagogue.

(Sonia)

In this chapter I look at the way the mothers interpreted and talked about their relationships with their children's school. Parent–school relationships, like much else that seizes popular attention, are cast in a negative light, and unfairly so. For millions of parents, the relationship is possibly the longest lasting and closest connection they'll ever have – approximately 11 years, when their children are 5–16. It is the one thing all parents have in common: the length of time their children are in compulsory education. All else is subject to their own personal history, education, time and philosophy about where they draw the line between home and school. Quite often two parents in the same household have different views on these variables. So my questions about communication were, unsurprisingly, interpreted in rather different ways. The questions with which I began this phase of our interaction were:

- what's your communication like with your child's school?
- do you get involved with anything going on at school?

- does being involved with school present any challenges?

These generic questions branched into an array of themes, of which the most common to emerge were: the positive ways in which the mothers were involved in school life and, in most cases, the ease of communication with staff. As several themes came up in the data, I have divided them across Chapters 5 and 6. This chapter deals with 'general' communication and challenges, while Chapter 6 explores specific academic-related engagement and obstacles, so distinguishing the macro from the micro. Barriers to the mothers' general relationships were more about feeling part of the school's community and less about the staff per se. Of course the school 'community' and staff are technically part of a shared space, but the data give insight into the nuanced way the two separate out – curds and whey.

Involvement in the school community

Trips, bazaars and events

The mothers' responses to the question about their involvement in school life highlight the range of ways they experienced positive participation. Key festival times such as the Christmas bazaar, Harvest festival collections and supporting Eid assemblies were listed as common annual events where they volunteered. Some found helping out in a classroom – listening to children reading, for example – a rewarding experience. The following comments represent what those involved felt:

> Every summer fair I volunteer, I've gone in to help with activities. I've tried to be part of the school community and I think it went really well.
>
> (Jameela)

> My kid's school makes a big effort. They do Eid, fun days, Diwali, assemblies on all the usual like Christmas and Harvest … they love diversity. I'm into supporting the tree planting project and raised money for it, doing henna. I do cakes for fundraising, I'm into the Macmillan cancer tea parties. I think we have to make an effort.
>
> (Erum, admin, L2)

> I've always been involved … helped with all the fairs, Christmas and summer, been to a lot of school trips. But now with my work times, my husband mostly goes. I've been a volunteer at the

school almost 5 years now, helping the teacher with admin stuff. And I work in a middle school too, that's been for four years.

(Mariam)

I did the most with my eldest … I'm not as involved now. I was chairperson of PTA for a quite a few years. Now I help when I can, but because of health issues and younger kids it's difficult. It was good for my kids to see that I was involved as well.

(Amira)

At primary school, I was there all the time. Secondary is different. I feel a bit, well, shy as I wasn't educated here and they might say something I don't follow. Just some words sometimes.

(Dina)

Dina listed her involvement with the Parent Teacher Association (PTA), listening to readers in class and successfully completing accredited English courses up to Level 2. Her narrative took a chronological approach that ended abruptly with secondary school, an experience common to most parents. In her case, Dina attributed the distance to the school's assumption that a higher level of intellectual and cultural capital is necessary to interact there.

In addition to participating in well-established ways, a few mothers discussed their offers to organize Eid-related activities. Two mothers recalled being specifically asked to do this. A few mothers had organized Eid assemblies, classroom activities or an exhibition. Their motivation was twofold: to support the teachers and to help the children feel proud of their heritage. The benefits of 'affirmation inclusion' – as Ipgrave (2010: 11) calls it – has positive repercussions for minority students in terms of their attendance and involvement at school.

Family liaison officers

Participation with parents was significantly increased by the presence of a family liaison/attendance officer. The community spokespersons of both focus groups discussed how coffee mornings and targeted activities such as parenting classes had a beneficial effect on their overall engagement. The relaxed atmosphere made the mothers feel comfortable to come in and share a particular problem, and on some occasions referrals to the right service providers have been made. In location 3, the presence of an attendance officer who spoke the same language as a significant proportion of the school's pupils, improved attendance and participation among both mothers and pupils in extracurricular activities.

Another way of getting involved in school life was by attending classes. Sumayyah had only lived in the UK for three years at the time of the interview. She attended Family Learning classes, despite having Masters-level qualifications in her home country. Sumayyah wanted to learn the techniques her children were being taught so she could support them more:

> I went into it because I wanted to know more, I didn't want to be left behind and it's helped me so much. I didn't understand the method of study, and then I learnt it all from Family Learning – 'help your child with numeracy and literacy' really helped me. And I've guided them and now they're the top students. I want to make sure they work hard and do their best.
>
> (Sumayyah, Qur'an teacher, L5)

Barriers

In and amongst accounts of the positive experience of forming relationships with their children's school, some interviews revealed a more complex picture, highlighting barriers to involvement. As the data shows, the examples come – ironically – from mothers who do participate, who have reflected on why they think parents may be reluctant to participate. The mothers who had a critical eye on their own communities shared certain biographical similarities – they were either professionally experienced in the education sector or had considerable experience through voluntary work in their local communities, or both. As we saw in Chapter 2, each mother's starting point affected their experience with the education sector, which had a layered effect on the data as a whole.

English language proficiency

About 10 of the 51 mothers needed a translator, as they couldn't communicate solely in English during the interviews. These included gatekeepers, other mothers, or myself, speaking Bangla and Urdu. Seven had no English at all and three switched between their mother tongue and English, which I mirrored by asking them the same questions in English and their home language. Overall, this allowed for a more authentic interview, rather than limiting their answers.

Despite controversy in public discourse – such as in the government press release titled '"Passive tolerance" of separate communities must end, says PM' (Department for Communities and Local Government, 2016) – for an increasing number of Muslim mothers the language factor is not an issue when they are interacting with schools. To help strengthen the home–school relationship, both locations where more help was needed had a dedicated member of staff such as a family link/attendance officer, who was from the same background as the mothers.

From my experience in adult education and family learning, I found that many parents, the majority of whom were mothers, made significant progress in their own lives and in building their confidence to engage with their child's education, by attending English classes. Conversely, a lack of proficiency in English, as one mother (Hodan) stated, leads to: 'parents behave[ing] angry and aggressive' and to this could be added, detached. The importance of learning English to a basic proficient level at least cannot be overemphasized. The 2011 census, which had a question on people's main language and self-assessed proficiency in English, showed that areas in London had a higher percentage of the population who categorized their English level as 'not good' or 'none at all' (ONS, 2013) compared to the national picture. However, a detailed analysis and breakdown of the figures – which age profiles are included and excluded, for example – is needed. For instance, are the non-proficient over 65-year-olds included? – there is a danger of thinking that certain communities have a bigger problem with English language than they do. This is but one part of the much more complex subject of illiteracy levels in adults nationally – which also affects parental engagement with schools.

Even with improvement, the language barrier manifests itself in other ways: through one's own children. Fahmida, a mother of four, who has Level 1 English proficiency, remarked: 'When there's something going on at school, my daughter, the eldest one says "don't come mum" because of my accent' and 'I feel shy because my English isn't that good' (Fahmida, L5). In spite of her child's discouragement, Fahmida regularly attended her local primary school's coffee afternoons, which gave her the confidence to volunteer at an after-school club. Clearly, confidence in speaking English is a vast subject. It was only partially discussed in one focus group, however, and given only a passing mention in two individual interviews. From my experience in English language teaching, where there is a culture of welcoming all parents into the school and a variety of ways for them to contribute, language is not a barrier, at least for some activities.

Self-reflection

Muslim families just leave them at school and don't want to know.

(Husna)

Some of them (South Asian parents) are very sheltered in this day and age. I don't know how. The world has changed ... but they haven't moved on.

(Emma)

I was a minority in the last school – it was all Pakistani and the way they were, it was too different, I didn't fit in and neither did my child.

(Catherine, teacher, L5)

I've been volunteering in a primary school 5 years. I have to say the majority of people who complain are Muslim mothers – it's always a Muslim mother ... and the school's got 50 per cent Muslim intake. Most of the time, what they complain about's nothing to do with religion, it's their culture. Like I don't complain about stuff as it's got nothing to do with religion. Seems like the more the school listens, the more they do it ... it's confusing for them [the school] ... what's culture and what's religion?

(Mariam)

A few mothers steered the discussion about their involvement with their children's school into a critical assessment of the Muslim community in their location. As the preceding quotes demonstrate, their criticisms were based on insularity, lack of engagement and a culture of complaining. The comments indicate the vast differences in the culture between those who were born and grew up in the UK and those who typically immigrated here quite recently, and who are therefore less inclined towards participation. Even this is only a generalization, as many variables affect the patterns of engagement. Dina blamed the extended family structure, for example, as did a few other mothers – four referred to living with their in-laws as a reason they couldn't get more involved with their children's school. While Dina herself, who came to the UK after marrying, was fully involved in her children's primary school, she confirmed that 'the joint family system makes it hard for some women' to do the same. Caring for the elderly and dealing with far larger numbers of relatives and family friends visiting is the way some families from traditional communities in the UK function.

The cultural differences were significant in all that was said, just as they are in real life. Emma and Catherine's perspectives are a common issue for English women who convert to Islam, traversing a cultural obstacle course in the process. For them location becomes a key issue and, as we saw in the discussions about school choice in Chapter 4, they take extra care to ensure that their children are not drowned in a Bangladeshi or Pakistani culture that was not part of their spiritual faith choice. Within our discussions, this was a lively subject of debate. Second-generation mothers with ethnic roots outside the UK join English Muslim women in redefining *their* identities – the online 'Muslim Mamas' group further emphasized this as a popular topic. Hybrid and hyphenated, whether they are British Muslim or British Pakistani Muslim, or something else, the 'constellation of Muslim identities' (Modood, 2007: 130) continues to rotate as it evolves in the UK.

The 'gap'

The lack of engagement by Muslim mothers was broached by a few participants, who acknowledged in an erudite way the complexity of barriers – identity, culture and class – in an attempt to explain exactly what they see and experience when it comes to communicating with schools. Bushra's discerning narrative explicitly captures what a few other mothers alluded to:

> Bushra: There seems to be a communication barrier, where many parents just make demands as they don't express themselves. So people like me get put together with them, and then we are asked to explain.
>
> SD: Do you mean explain on their behalf?
>
> B: Yes, because I think there's a gap. If I talk to them (teachers) about something, then they'll ask me something else – unrelated, but they wouldn't approach me and ask before as they're scared to offend. So it comes across like staff don't understand, or they've got a harsh attitude, but actually it's because there's a gap … a gap between parents and school.
>
> SD: Is there a particular example that comes to mind?
>
> B: It was in December, I felt that I needed to go in and explain to her I don't mind my child participating in the Christmas play, just not acting as Mary and have a word about lyrics in some hymns. I explained it to her and it was a lovely conversation as I could explain things she didn't know even though she was head at a previous school with over half of the intake of Muslim children, and she never understood why children missed Christmas assembly. She said no-one's ever explained any of this to her and we looked over the Qur'an passages where Mary is

mentioned. Then from that she asked why Pakistani people take so many holidays. I explained I'm born here and not Pakistani people's representative, but we need to have that conversation later. It seems like there's a communication problem with the parents who don't articulate themselves but make demands, so when I come along they want to know.

Several points arise from such data: how does information flow? Who is perceived as approachable and who is not? To solve the problem of the 'demanding' or 'angry' parent ironically requires education. These tensions and struggles, familiar to anyone – parents or staff working in the unique microcosm of society that a state school is – show just how messy is the task of unpicking stereotypes, faith and culture to help staff understand the differences. Aside from these themes and away from the strictures of predetermined phenomena, the nuances of what was said, half-said and unsaid echo a clear message: more communication between schools, communities and parents is required if we are to ensure that the holistic wellbeing of children is the motivating factor in all we do.

Festivals

The topic of general communication led some mothers to discuss cultural programmes and festivals. They revealed that they had an ongoing dialogue with certain teachers about their own culture, as in Zainab's example:

> My interaction with teachers was mostly academic. But some teachers asked me about cultural practices and cultural enlightenment. I used to say I was from India and teachers were surprised ... some knew our state was top of the world for women's literacy.

Given the scaremongering in the media (GLA, 2006) over the past two decades about Muslims' reaction to Christmas, among this diverse sample of women the festival was not regarded as a major problem in their child's schooling. Other comments about festivals were made in the context of wider, across-faith celebrations, and took an inclusive approach:

> I want my children to learn about all religions, all festivals ... Harvest, Diwali, Chinese New Year, all of it. That's part of their education. I support all the trips.

> (Mariam)

Regular school festivals such as Easter, Harvest and Christmas were mentioned by just under half of the mothers and mostly in passing. Five had spoken to the class teacher about their child not acting in the role of Mary or Jesus. This view comes from the widely accepted stance across the Muslim community of not drawing or imitating prophets or revered people from the sacred texts. Two of the five included the subject of hymns in conversations with their child's class teacher, explaining that while in Christianity Jesus is called the son of God, in Islam he is a Prophet of God. Neither mother withdrew her child, saying they simply wanted the teacher to know if their child missed out those words, there was a reason based on Muslim beliefs. There was a consensus individually and in the group that schools encourage learning about all religions as part of the curriculum: 'They know what a church is, a synagogue is … that's all fine, they do them in religious lessons. They've been to them too, a church and synagogue' (Sonia, admin, L1).

Notably, none of the mothers in either focus group raised the subject of festivals. This could be because they had more pressing priorities or because the focus groups had to accommodate multiple opinions in a limited time, which might have reduced each participant's opportunity to say all she wanted to say. Nonetheless, those who did speak about it had a few points they felt needed to be heard.

For some of the mothers, the main concern was halal sweets and snacks at the Christmas party. They emphasized that very young children didn't ask whether sweets contained gelatine and that the parents needed to communicate this. There were differences in the ways schools conducted Christmas parties, and how these mothers felt about this. In one school, for example, Christmas was celebrated by 'a disco with loud pop music'. One mother felt this would be uncomfortable for her son and discussed whether he might miss it with his teacher. The range of views is similar to that found in Scourfield *et al.*'s (2013) study of 60 Muslim families, which explored how they cultivated faith and religious practice – from full engagement to exercising caution – in their children's lives (2013: 173–6).

By contrast, Sonia reflected on her own feelings as a child, when she longed to join in with Christmas celebrations that never took place at home. Her choices for her children were based on her childhood memories, hence her efforts to ensure her children don't feel the same disappointment.:

Sonia: My nephew's had a Halloween disco at his school. Some parents think it's wrong. But I don't. If they know what's right and wrong, then it's alright. It's about getting into the festivity, about respecting.

SD: Respecting cultures, maybe?

S: Yeah, if you want them to respect your culture, then you have to respect theirs. And it's just getting into the festivity of it. I remember when I was at primary school and I'd put a sock on the heater, thinking Santa's going to come ... but he didn't. So this time, I had a Christmas tree, even though everyone frowned on me. It's for them. So they can go back and say I had a Christmas tree and be a part of it, like have the dinner and stuff. Well they're old enough to understand.

SD: Who frowned on it?

S: Just some friends and some family, people who want to push their views on to me. But it's my decision. It's like I'm not worshiping it, it's just a tree. The tree was just there, we still prayed and went to mosque. Like I went to a Halloween party. The kids got dressed up and my in-laws were like that's wrong – that's dressing up like devils. But it's up to me though, isn't it? You could say I'm a rebel – a rebel mum.

Ribbens *et al.*'s discussion of the 'considerable variability between mothers in terms of how far they may expect continuity or sharp differentiation in a child's experience between the home and the school' (2005: 70) sheds some light on Sonia's comments. Her mixture of school, home, respect for cultures and her own past blur the distinction between the supposedly independent spheres of her and her children's lives. For another mother, who spoke repeatedly of 'fitting in' throughout her interview, festivals, food and exchanging information was a way to help her daughter's identity be accepted:

My daughter was the first Muslim child at her primary school, and there were a lot of issues about saying here name, it wasn't a problem – the teachers just asked me a few times, and, like her surname's Arabic ... it's hard. But we had no real issues at all.

I remember in reception, the teacher asked me about Eid and what you do, we lent them some easy books. They had an Eid festival. Once when there was a food tasting day the teacher kindly stopped me and asked if this or that was alright. We did have discussions about what she can and can't eat – like sweets in the book bag and after parties.

(Emma)

Communication between parents

Interaction between parents at the school gate is guided by a set of laws unique to each school's community. When they saw communication with the school in terms of belonging and feeling part of the community, their thoughts extended into this area, as the extracts below indicate. In some cases there were subtle divisions. Wahida's account is part of a longer narrative in which she explores the problems associated with wanting to be part of the school community but finds that other parents' attitudes and possible perceptions require careful consideration on a daily basis:

> Sometimes it felt unfair ... not because the friends are Muslims or Asian, it's because we get on – that's why I'd talk to them. But this ... it's unfair that you have baggage on you all the time. The English mums can talk to who they want and just be ... but maybe I'm overthinking it ... and you can't just, you know ... you have to make that effort. Sometimes it doesn't get you anywhere. The chair of the PTA would ask for help, and I'd always put my name down and she'd never contact me. Then I'd ring her and say it and then get a chance. So sometimes you have to make double the effort.
>
> (Wahida)

'Double the effort' sums up the management of relationships; of making them, of embodying a counter-narrative on a daily basis in the playground, of projecting oneself as approachable, of avoiding falling into the mass-produced stereotypes – this is the work these mothers take on when they want to integrate and are looking to contribute. Below, Nasra and others speak about how the already fragile relationship building takes on other dimensions:

> Every summer fair I volunteer, I've gone in to help with activities. I've tried to be part of the school community, and I think it went really well, in terms of my child and their friends – who will say hello to me and know me and in terms of their class teachers. But I had to make more of an effort to fit in ... for instance – when they're making things in the PTA – alcohol is a big issue – every occasion has alcohol. I would have loved to join the mothers, but because they said all bring a drink along, it was outside what I'm prepared to do.
>
> (Jameela)

As I run a small business, some of my clients are also parents. On a business level there's no problem communicating. One client was fine online and on email and everything. But when he saw me in the playground he acted like he didn't know me. Well I'm wearing a scarf, it's obvious I'm Muslim.

(Nasra)

I'll admit Mums feel rejection – no one's socially forthcoming until they know your child has passed the 11+. There are types of Muslim mums – those enclosed in their own world and don't deal with what's going on. But for the ones that want to get involved, these mums feel activities need to be 'inclusive'. For example, there was a primary school festival and it was based around music and beer. The faith boundaries I have just won't allow this.

(Saba)

Several matters arise from these quotes that require further attention. Race dynamics and ethno-religious identities, cultural practices and the symbolism in outer appearance converge into invisible boundaries between integration and separation. This combination raises more questions than space allows me to answer. Any thought of a 'solution' may exist in a utopian land where people from diverse backgrounds congregate twice a day on charcoal tarmac and, in the process of collecting their child from a classroom, find commonalities, forge friendships, embrace differences and create a vibrant community. This is certainly achieved by some schools that have invested in building an inclusive and supportive environment.

Within their narratives, the women offered explanations for their experiences: the deeply negative image of Islam, Muslims and Muslim women held by the dominant group, and sustained through regular stories in the press. Saba rationalized the negativity as a combination of the following: the view that some migrants are lazy because they can't find work, the fact that historically they have been insular and not integrated, plus the media image of angry, violent extremists. Together this has led some parents to avoid any contact with them. Saba went on to say that only 'exceptional achievements, like your child passing the 11+, changes their attitude and then they'll speak to you'. Other mothers thought that parents' fear of the unknown led to mistaken assumptions, particularly when coupled with popular stereotypes and current news stories:

And if you are friends, like I was with this mum for over a year … as in, we had playdates, and we'd been to each other's houses

... then the guard comes down and one day she asked me: 'how d'you feel about having a forced marriage?'

I nearly spluttered my tea out and said 'Do you mean forced marriage or arranged marriage?' 'No, forced,' she said. This is after a year of solid friendship and she'd met my husband several times, and I'd met hers. I explained that I met my husband through a friend, it was 'arranged' by everyone, but not forced, as I agreed to it. Even though she knew me, she still asked me this question as she had assumptions in her head. That week, they were bringing in laws against forced marriage and it was in the news. And everything that's in the news comes out in the playground. She said what everyone else is thinking and felt she could ask because we were friends.

(Bushra)

The struggle of living one's daily life when faced with generalizations from news stories is at the centre of what Bushra says. Her story is all the more unsettling as one would expect that her personal agency – something she emphasizes at the beginning of her account – should have been enough to ensure that she was treated like anyone else, as normal. As Bushra's account demonstrates, normal – whatever that means – is something of a luxury. Parallels may be drawn to Kaye Haw's study (1998) about the lives of Muslim girls in the late 1990s. Haw heard similar accounts from the teenage girls in a city in northern England. Her widely quoted analysis speaks of a dual effect of the media. In a similar way to the mothers here, the girls in her study internalized the negative media stories affecting their peers. This is a layer that both the teenage girls then and the mothers in their early thirties now contend with. Saeed (2007) discusses the relationship between Muslims and the media and acknowledges that 'voices in the media and politicians' are imploring them to make a more strenuous effort to integrate (2007: 453). There was a feeling from my participants, however, that as much as they want to integrate, their efforts are counterproductive because the media has foreshadowed their identity, predetermining and fixing who they are. This is evident in what they say about the playground politics, about the questions they're asked, the avoidances that are made, the struggles they choose to engage in, or not. Such encounters are often so subtle and nuanced that to all other eyes there is nothing going on. The women strive to assert their ordinariness but find that 'acceptance' requires something extraordinary. As Saba exclaimed: 'You have to be Mo Farah or something to be respected ... like something else, off the radar!'

The following extract gives an aerial view of the subtle segregation taking place in a school (Type A) whose population has become more diverse. While the change might have been managed smoothly inside the school, beyond the classrooms there was a tectonic shift. The mother narrating was in a unique position to 'see' the situation, being both Muslim and English:

Emma: Then when more Muslim mums started coming to the school there was a bit of a hoo-ha as they'd congregate and not mix with the others. And the Muslim mums decided they'd stop standing in small groups and talk to everyone instead, but it took a while to sort out. The playground has been one place that's upset me, it's not the teaching, it's not the teachers, it's about fitting in. It can be very nasty, it can, the playground.

SD: What was the hoo-ha about?

E: After about a couple of years, some families started at the school. The school was asking me how to deal with it. I thought I can't see all this ... but when I stood back and looked, actually I could see it. Some of the white mums were being rude about Muslim families coming into the village, whether it's an outsider thing – like someone coming from the town to the village and taking 'our' school places, or a covering issue – like not understanding it and religion ... I don't know. ... I think what happened, is that the Muslim families came in a group ... and I did hear the word 'invasion', and I remember saying to some of the mums, I go to the same mosque, and they're lovely ladies.

SD: What did the school think you could do?

E: I suppose I was asked because I said I knew them. The headteacher was more than happy to have them but was getting worried about issues ... like the playground. Because I was helping in the PTA, I was seen as the 'Muslim voice'.

Parent governor roles

In the UK the school governor role is a voluntary position whereby local citizens can be elected into office. There are categories of governors: staff, local authority, parent and community. The role of the governor is to hold the school accountable for its policies and general running. They do not evaluate teaching standards as this is the remit of Ofsted. As stated in the DfE booklet (2014) on guidance to school governors:

> [Governors] are the strategic leaders of our schools and have a vital role to play in making sure every child gets the best possible education. For maintained schools this is reflected in the law, which states that the 6 purposes of maintained school governing bodies is to conduct the school with a view to promoting high standards of educational achievement at the school.

Governors are expected to bring valuable skills to the governing body, which will assist with the various committees. Parent governors make a significant contribution in the UK. A longstanding issue with parent governor recruitment has been the lack of diversity, particularly when governing bodies are encouraged or required to be representative of the school's demographic. Accordingly studies and surveys have looked at representation.

The Runnymede briefing paper (Rollock, 2009), which looked at all governors' engagement with issues of race equality and community cohesion, notes the range of experiences for Black–African and Caribbean governors, who along with other under-represented groups feel alienated from aspects of the governing body.

The fact that governors usually tend to be white and middle class has also been cited as a hindrance to making governing bodies more diverse (Rollock, 2009; Ellis, 2009). Research exploring the experiences of Black governors around issues of recruitment and retention found that they felt that challenging this prevailing – white, middle-class – image was important to encouraging those from Black and minority ethnic groups to become governors.

The position of the mothers in my study varied from being involved in multiple voluntary boards to feeling disillusioned because of their lack of agency. Rizwana was a parent governor at a highly diverse school but there was little representation of ethnic minorities on the governing body. She also chaired a community group of parents to support children with special needs in the local health authority and played an active role as a mother of three young children on top of her part-time work in schools. Others spoke of the challenges they faced alongside their desire to make a contribution to school life. The dilemmas of different roles are apparent in the following extract:

> I always felt it was important to contribute. I wouldn't call it pressure. I felt like I couldn't sit there and be silent ... an observer. It's almost like I had to prove I was worthy of being there. I was a governor in a mixed school in an all-white middle-class

governing body. I was the Asian, woman governor. I believe I was there for the school, not the Asians and not for the Muslims. I felt, if I'm perfectly honest, I didn't feel welcome. I don't know whether it's because I was different, not what they expected ... they were sussing out why I was there. Although I didn't enjoy being a governor for a long time, I felt it was important for me to do it. They kept on going on about the need to have an 'ethnic minority'. But, if I felt like that, how could I sell it to anyone else, like 'come and feel uncomfortable too'! I don't know whether it's cliquiness and they're similar. I would go in and be polite and say hello to everyone, and it was really strange ... then you question, if it's me? ... is it me, am I just seeing things that aren't there? If I didn't say hello, then someone else wouldn't say hello to me – it was just little things like that. I was involved in other ways though, I did assemblies, regularly ... throughout primary and I still go in and give talks even though I'm not a governor anymore. And I've done loads with the PTA. They approach me to do the samosa order.

(Tahira)

Tahira's account indicates the barriers to governance found in Ellis's study (Ellis, 2009). This set out to understand how six groups – disabled, ethnic minority, those on low incomes, women, young people and lone parents – experienced volunteering and specifically school governance. While there is an important discussion on the lack of strategies for ethnic minority governor recruitment across local authorities, the study's finding on barriers is of direct relevance here. For example:

A number of respondents felt that other members of their governing body held prejudiced or stereotypical views towards certain minority groups of people (whether that group be defined by ethnicity, age, social class or disability). These views were resulting in people feeling marginalised within their governing body.

(Ellis, 2009: 49)

Notably, my study's participants listed several practical and experiential obstacles to becoming a governor and enjoying the role: language barriers, childcare costs and having an inadequate understanding of the British education system. For those mothers in my study who were also governors, none of these obstacles was the reason they found governance a difficult experience. The experience Jameela relates illustrates the nuanced way a variety of issues cross-cut one another:

> Jameela: I found them paying lip service to things like diversity and equalities and different cultures on the part of management, less on the part of staff – they tried to translate the teaching of cultures in the classroom. But there was definitely less enthusiasm from above and that goes across cultures. It's a continuous struggle, not getting info, meeting times, not having emails returned. Like it's not their responsibility to have equalities policy done – even though it is their responsibility. I've had to work hard to get diverse speakers in, as they're comfortable with the mono-culture.
>
> The attitude's a struggle, not just in the governing body. It's in the playground too – it's the same. It's very distinct, even fellow governors won't speak to you in the playground, except if their child wants your child over to play – it's for their child, not for themselves.
>
> SD: Does this have any impact on how your children fit in?
>
> J: My children get invited over a lot less than others. For play 70 per cent of their invites are from non-English (European and others), 30 per cent English. The younger one has no other ethnic groups in his class so not invited over at all. There's a real difference between parents from one class to another. It's not what I'm looking for, it's in my face. With my daughter where there's a mix, parents will talk, with the other one – no one will speak to me.
>
> Every summer fair I volunteer, I've gone in to help with activities. I've tried … I've tried to be part of the school community. I think it went really well, in terms of one child and their friends – who will say hello to me and know me and their class teachers.
>
> (Jameela)

Jameela's account details the way two areas cut across each other: the experience of being a governor and the playground politics around ethnicity. She sees the playground politics as an extension of the governance – the exclusion where there should be inclusion. Jameela's narrative echoes those from mothers who had some position of authority in the school.

It demonstrates the intricacy of handling the personal role as a mother alongside fulfilling the public role of a governor. There are no neat boxes to demarcate emotions and resilience, alongside the desire to become part of the community. The concept of emotional capital is helpful. In Reay's (2000) exploration of emotional capital based on maternal involvement in their children's schooling during the 1990s, she unearthed the complex ways positive and negative emotions affected their children and 'the cost to mothers of their emotional involvement in their children's schooling. They are using up a lot of time and energy in their support' (2000: 578). Here, in Jameela's case, her emotional capital works to find a space for her children and herself to be part of the school community and feel accepted.

The other theme that surfaces in this extract is how the equality and diversity policy is viewed. The need for diversity when most of the pupils are white and middle class may seem a low priority from one perspective; the status quo does not 'feel' the consequences of a mono-culture. The same can – and should – be applied to schools where ethnic minorities dominate and white British children and their parents feel the sense of alienation, as we have seen. Neither situation helps community cohesion at a policy level, nor, more importantly, do they bode well for basic human relationships.

The mothers who have been parent governors expressed the difficulty they, as confident women, nonetheless experience. Successful, graduate mothers, multi-skilled, bilingual, who have lived all their adult lives in the UK, found it difficult to feel accepted and comfortable in the governing body. How, then, do the policies they are supposed to enforce – such as promoting community cohesion and inclusion – become authentic solutions? There is something of an anomaly if the very people who need to be *on* governing bodies experience being subtly sidelined.

Each of the three themes explored in this chapter exemplify the intersectional way ethnicity, faith, gender and class overlap and elucidate minority positions. My reflective notes drew on a comparison after the interviews that I have presented here. Although casual conversations made me aware of the challenges and positive participation mothers experienced, I had not anticipated their feelings of marginality, which came across in some the extracts I have used in this chapter. I compared what I heard to an old file, from 2006, when in the thick of my own parent–school involvement, personally and professionally, I conducted a small survey at a Muslim women's parenting weekend. The attendees were a cross-section of Muslim women from across the UK, with a higher-than-average proportion of English converts. Other than that they were a random sample. The survey attempted to capture the parents' experiences of school life for their children through short questions, answered on a sliding scale, with space to write their own comments. The survey was intended to inform and improve CPD sessions I was delivering on Islam Awareness for my colleagues at the time. Approximately 38 mothers of school-going children completed the survey after one of the seminars. Their main concerns were about their child's faith being understood, marking special occasions such as Eid assemblies and staff having a basic understanding of the main Muslim beliefs – especially where a school's percentage of Muslim children is high.

A decade later, the landscape has changed. Geopolitics, policies on minorities, the increased use of the language of securitization, have all led to concerns about increased segregation and diminished cohesion, according to some mothers' experiences. The fact that these are a few amongst hundreds and thousands of voices should not negate the importance of what they are saying. Chapter 6 takes the broad issues in this chapter and drills down to certain specifics.

Who's watching who?
Parents'evening, SRE and security

I don't go in to school. They're alright, teachers help. I go on my own for parents' evening though.

(Samira)

At this stage ... we're just trying to understand what the system is, how it's running.

(Dina)

Our parents found all that difficult to explain. I think it's good for them to get that help from teachers.

(Naila)

I have to think a hundred ways before I bring something up. Which way will it be taken, this way, that way, will it cause more trouble, will they make assumptions about my child, will this go down as 'extreme', who defines what's extreme?

(Nasra)

In this chapter I present the mothers' answers to the questions about communication and their relationship with their child's school, as outlined in Chapter 5. The marked differences in their responses flags up the immense social and cultural variety of their lives and attitudes. By delving deeper into their experiences, this chapter highlights specific challenges in communication – about their child's academic performance, for example – and their experiences of parents' evening. Within the curriculum, the subject reported to be most 'challenging' was Sex and Relationship Education (SRE). The final section of the chapter discusses legislation passed at the time of the interviews that caused a number of mothers to raise the topic of surveillance in the context of the government's Preventing Violent Extremism (PVE) strategy.

Parents' evening and academic progress

All the mothers I interviewed individually thought that attending parents' evening was a priority, whether or not they struggled with English. A few said their language skills were better than their husband's, so it was they who always attended. Other strategies used when communication might be an issue was to take a friend, have another member of staff present or rely on their child – in secondary school in particular – to help with translation, although this posed ethical issues.

There was general agreement in both focus groups that parents' evening was important 'to listen to what the teacher had to say and compare that to what my children have been saying' (Fatima, homemaker, L3). Where there was a disagreement between what a teacher and a child said, the mothers in location 4 concurred with Huda: 'I'll believe what the teacher says over my child; 'cos our kids act different one way at home and are totally different at school – that's what I think anyway' (Huda). There were some caveats, however, as in Tahira's caution:

> But it's important not to think they know who your child is. In one school where there were lots of Asians, the teacher didn't know who my son was and was talking about someone else entirely. You can't assume they know. You have to ask if something doesn't sound right. I know my children.
>
> (Tahira)

Being intensively supportive

A few mothers described in detail their deliberate efforts to support their children's academic progress. They knew their levels and the new timetabling system and checked the work they were set online – even what the children are given to eat – using the parent online system. Persistence characterized the mothers' narratives: they contacted the school in person or by telephone as often as required to see their child make progress – by *their* standards:

> I provide them support after school. I buy the books online and York notes. Teachers can only do a certain amount. You have to work hard to get the grades and there are more distractions nowadays. I make sure she reads the York notes, and they have online parent place and I look at what homework they've got, or if they're late for lessons.
>
> (Husna)

Husna believed that the communication with her daughter's school was positive and welcoming. She had been thanked by one of the teachers for her joint effort in improving the results for an exam her daughter was retaking. Husna, a full-time working mother, made no less than four sixth form applications to guarantee that her daughter's A-level studies continued at the best institution to ensure university entrance and a career. Her efforts compare to those used by the ethnic minority parents in Louise Archer's study (2010), who utilized their capitals to avert the effects of low expectations and in some cases stereotyping. By taking control from the outset, Husna's strategy seems to leave no room for low expectations. At the other end of the education system, Dina is equally assiduous in her strategy for her children, who are at primary school:

> At this stage … we're just trying to understand what the system is and how it runs. When they got to primary school I wanted them to have the best opportunity and I'm always in there asking. If I give you a[n] example, if I get a report that I'm not happy with … I don't feel comfortable about the national levels and if I think my child is capable of being higher than their guidelines then this is the biggest issue, to get them support and push and push. … You know English levels are so high now, and high expectations, it's so hard to achieve now. Like my daughter had a level 3B at the end of Year 3 and I had a big problem with that.
>
> (Dina)

Some of the mothers, like Tahira, linked their involvement with their children's academic progress to resisting essentialized views of themselves. Unlike a book, people's real lives are not separated thematically, and in Tahira's case, differentiating herself as an involved mother endowed with educational capital resonated throughout her interview, rising and falling, yet persistent:

> I go to parents' evenings and once I realized she'd mixed my son up with someone else … are all Asian children the same? I always go because I want to hear and I want them to see me … that I want the best, and they need to know. And I want them to know I'm eloquent and fluent in English, as they make assumptions that if you wear a scarf or dress a certain way … it's saying we're not all the same. There have been occasions where teachers have said some things that don't sit right. I feel I know my children, if they say they're going to enter him for a lower level, say, then I'll have a conversation with the teacher and with my child and I'll listen to my children.

> I know for a fact that a lot of Asian parents don't go to parents' evening. I feel like I've got to prove my point that I'm concerned, I've got a mission and purpose … I make it clear I'm concerned and ask a lot of questions. I do the whole smartly dressed thing. I need to show them I'm educated.
>
> (Tahira)

Both Dina and Tahira's extracts reveal similarities to Sharon Hays' popular concept of 'intensive mothering' (1996). The way in which their intensity manifests differs to the examples in Hays' study, but their professional approach nonetheless corresponds to the intensive mothering dynamic. In Dina's case, the intensity could be attributed to her aspirations for her children and a desire to overcome any hurdles she anticipates, particularly because she feels a lack of familiarity with the education system, having studied outside the UK.

Sooner rather than later

Tangentially linked to parents' evening was the opinion of a few mothers that this official route of exchanging information was often a case of too little too late when their child was having problems they were unaware of. They felt that home–school communication was generally good as long as their child was making academic progress. When problems became apparent only at the annual meeting, the mothers felt let down – which could be a general problem unrelated to ethnicity or faith. They noted that the way teachers have to use positive, euphemistic language when communicating with parents doesn't always reflect the true picture – until the child is underperforming and problems are deeply entrenched:

> He went down two levels, and if they'd told me before then I'd do something about it. When I did find out then I had words with him and like, then gradually he went up two levels. But I wish I'd known earlier.
>
> (Sonia)

> Communication with secondary school is a challenge: two were like closed doors, only open for parents' evening. I think if you're having negative feedback, like they're not behaving, or it's academic progress – it's not easy. But, what we wanted to know is why weren't we told at the outset, not when it's too late.
>
> (Asma)

It's difficult to know when to speak with secondary school. It depends who the teacher is.

(Kausar, English as a Second Language student, L5)

SRE

Discussion of the challenges the mothers faced turned to the theme of sex and relationship education (SRE) as it is taught in UK primary and secondary schools. Over the years parents' voices and the schools' teaching of SRE has been portrayed as a contentious, sensitive subject, particularly as there are deep-rooted values attached to esoteric moral and ethical ideas of what is appropriate and inappropriate. Researching people's experiences and views requires paying as much attention to what is not said as to what is. Interestingly, 24 of the mothers – almost half – named SRE as a subject they find challenging. In the focus groups, once one of them raised the subject half of them started speaking about it. The others spoke about SRE in individual interviews, in ways that reflected their children's ages and upbringing. There are several possible reasons why 27 mothers did not mention SRE, including the age of their children. For the very young, or those reaching the end of Key Stage 4, the subject is either too remote or no longer relevant. Or the mothers might possibly be satisfied with the way they or the school, or both, are handling the subject. Mothers might also be silent about it if they are less aware of curriculum content or not closely engaged. A few in location 2 had little experience of education in the UK, which could explain their reticence.

The mothers' words reveal the disconnect in some cases between the school's policy, how SRE is taught and parents' knowledge about it all. Others voiced support for SRE that is taught in an age-appropriate way and respects faith-centred values. Part of the problem parents face is confusion about what exactly constitutes SRE and where the subject stands in the curriculum.

SRE is a strand of the broader curriculum area known as Personal Social Health Education (PSHE) and is currently non-statutory in primary school. The only legal elements of SRE at Key Stage 2 are its links to the science curriculum, which covers the stages of human physical development into puberty and adulthood, in the context of life cycles. At secondary level, during Key Stage 3 only – school years 7–9 – state-maintained schools are required to teach SRE, which includes, according to DfES statutory guidance, reproduction, sexuality and sexual health (DfE, 2013a). Academies and free schools in the UK are not legally obliged to follow the National Curriculum, but still teach the subject, most commonly through the science curriculum. Biology syllabi and associated teaching materials in the first three years of secondary education cover reproduction.

More important than the biological aspects, some would argue, is the context of personal, social and health education. According to DfE (2013b) guidance:

> Schools should seek to use PSHE to build, where appropriate, on the statutory content already outlined in the national curriculum, the basic school curriculum and in statutory guidance on: drug education, financial education, sex and relationship education (SRE) and the importance of physical activity and diet for a healthy lifestyle.

This PSHE has a wide-reaching remit, addressing several legal duties – for instance, children's wellbeing, community cohesion and safeguarding – placed on schools. It also provides a holistic platform from which topics related to SRE can be tackled.

Educationalists have expressed longstanding concerns over the delivery of PSHE – and by association SRE – as provision varies in quantity and quality from school to school. Teachers who deliver SRE cite training and resources as an issue, as there are no performance indicators measuring the progress made in this area of the curriculum (Mason, 2010). Compounding the problem is the reality that a generation of young people – unlike any before them – have limitless access to adult information and websites on the internet. Senior management in schools has the tall-order task of not only deciding on the content but staying abreast of young people's rapidly changing lives online, even when they're in primary school. Social media sites with age limits are easily contravened; several underage children admit to having accounts on popular sites three or four years below the permitted age.

Reflecting the importance of these two curriculum areas, the report of the House of Commons Education Committee (2015) made several recommendations to improve the provision of PSHE and SRE. Most pertinent were those that included: reinstating PSHE CPD for teachers, better engagement with parents on SRE provision, renaming the subject to RSE to reflect the priority of relationship education and taking a holistic approach:

> We recommend that Ofsted set out clearly in the school inspection handbook the way in which a school's PSHE provision relates to

Ofsted's judgements on safeguarding and pupils' spiritual, moral, social and cultural development.

(House of Commons Education Committee, 2015: 46)

Mason's study found considerable differences in the provision of SRE in two rural, mono-cultural primary schools. School A provided a single lesson on body changes while School B provided one lesson a week for 6 weeks that built up children's knowledge of body changes and conception. School A did not communicate with parents; school B did. The research captured a sample of children's responses before and after regular SRE lessons and found that the teachers' confidence and creativity during regular lessons increased the children's holistic understanding of body changes and relationships. This was not the case for the children who received only one lesson.

The matter of parents and SRE is contentious. The DfES directive states that parents have the right to withdraw their children from non-statutory parts of the lessons. Debates centre on the failure of parents to address the subject when they do withdraw their children, the difference in values around relationships between schools, and the way faith or belief systems can conflict with the school ethos. However, the Education Committee's report endorses, amongst several recommendations, the parent's part in SRE:

> Parental engagement is key to maximising the benefits of SRE. The Government should require schools to consult parents about the provision of SRE, and ask Ofsted to inspect the way in which schools do this. The existing right of a parent to withdraw their child from elements of SRE must be retained.

(House of Commons Education Committee, 2015: 5)

Faith schools have traditionally been criticized over their teaching of SRE. However, a 2013 Ofsted report highlighted the case of a Catholic school as exemplary in the way SRE was taught:

> The school works with parents and carers from the start of transition from primary to secondary school to build valued relationships of trust and respect. It is by establishing such relationships that SRE can be taught openly and effectively [...] SRE is valued by the governing body [...] PSHE education is a whole-school development priority and the staff responsible for planning and delivering SRE are able to have confident and open discourse and discussion with the governors to address pertinent and relevant issues within the subject. This commitment by

governors signals the importance of good provision for SRE to the whole school community.

(Ofsted, 2012)

The themes expressed in the following comments summarize the points that recurred most in the interview data. The first extracts point to parents' need to know what is actually being delivered, when and how. Those who received information discussed how they responded. Both focus group discussions showed clearly that parents with children in the same school had varying levels of knowledge about what is delivered. During the focus group in location 2, views were gathered by going around the group to give everyone a chance to speak, rather than allowing the more vocal mothers to speak on behalf of the rest. The comments were therefore brief:

> H: We as parents need to see what is shown.

> L: We don't know what they're taught, we don't get invited. The kids are so shy, they don't say it.

> E: We haven't had the opportunity to see the video in Year 6. We want to see the contents of what they show.

> J: Do they show videos? I don't know ... do they here?

> I: If we know, we can relate to it, and we know what they're talking about.

> N: Our parents found it difficult to explain. I think it's good for them to get that help from teachers. I like it coming from both sides. I'm studying child development myself ... and what they do at school's helped me, as I knew what to expect.

* * *

In location 3's focus group, the following exchange with one participant speaks for the rest of the group, who generally shunned the principle of teaching SRE in primary school:

> Fatima: If it was up to me, I would not teach it, and now I've heard there's a video, I would like to know when do they show that?

> SD: Would you watch the video if you had the opportunity?
> F: Neither me nor my children want to see it.

A discussion ensued about letters going home, but these mothers had no knowledge of such letters, or whether SRE is taught in Year 4 or Year 5. Fatima resumed:

> Fatima: My child said they didn't show them video.
>
> Hodan: They used to seek our consent and send a letter but now no one seeks our consent. The children are young. Is it Year 4 or Year 3?
>
> Amaal: Sex education starts at Year 3. I don't know what type of video they watch but my daughter came home with things I don't agree with.
>
> I didn't have to talk to the school when she was in primary. There was a form and I ticked the box saying I didn't want her to go to it. There was a choice. For me I didn't need to know till I had to. Yes, she'll know about it from me, or when she wants to know. I think it's taking her innocence away – it's not necessary. Now in secondary, I recently had letters through about this subject. I said to her, you're gonna have this, if you have questions come and ask me.
>
> (Nilofer)

* * *

> Mariam: SRE was a bit of a challenge. There was only two of us parents who stopped our children from seeing the videos. I went to see the videos and said no way I'm letting my daughter see this. I recommend every parent should go and watch it. So then, I took my son and daughter aside and explained to them, but my son didn't want to know! I explained to the school and they were very understanding. I suggested they could have this lesson on a Friday afternoon so kids can go home and talk it over the weekend and forgot about it by Monday.
>
> Huda: Yeah, similar to Mariam. For my son, I didn't let him see the video, as I went first and decided for my child at the age of 10, I didn't think he was mentally ready.
>
> SD: Did you tell the school?

> Huda: I did. I said to them, that he's not ready – at least I'm his mother and I know him and that's what I think. And they were good about it, like Mariam said … about when they showed it and the day and all that. But he did the rest of the lesson.

* * *

These comments illustrate how difficult it was for those mothers who didn't feel informed, and the challenges for those who had some form of dialogue with the school. The spectrum of views and strategies is only a sample of what was said, but it is representative. The first focus group discussion shows, however, that there is a point at which the school input is appreciated alongside the parent's efforts. That particular mother's background also shaped how she reacted to the subject – as we've seen, different starting points elicit different responses. Mothers from sub-Saharan Africa, for example, would be familiar with sex education as 'family-life education' or 'life-skills education' (Chilisa, 2006: 250). With the exception of a few mothers who knew about content and 'managing' the teaching of SRE, the recurring concept of *hayaa* – translated as 'modesty, appropriateness, natural inclination' – was the single common thread that ran through the data on SRE. A common Islamic concept, *hayaa* can be understood as what is appropriate, modest behaviour. It is closely aligned to safeguarding in terms of protecting children's rights. A prophetic saying places *hayaa* as part of one's faith (*Iman*) thus: *Iman consists of more than sixty branches and hayaa (modesty) is a part of faith* (Sahih Bukhari).

For example, in Muslim culture a child over 7 has the right not to be observed while changing, showering or using the bathroom; their rights to privacy as they get older are an understood part of their growing up, as is the privacy of the adults around them. The following comments show mothers being proactive about teaching their children and managing how much they knew, and at what age.

Proactive about SRE

> We had letters sent out, and I went to the consultation. I didn't agree with some bits. I said I'd teach my child. I know a lot of families don't, like my parents didn't. With my daughter I can say I was OK that they've got compulsory education on growth and babies, but not the rest, like using contraception in Year 7. I wrote a letter for my son and said I don't believe my son's ready yet and when he is we can get him the information.

For us it's about *hayaa*, like modesty – he doesn't feel comfortable. I did discuss it with him, he was happy, he didn't want to go. There were only two Muslims in the class and he didn't feel comfortable. I know it's National Curriculum, but certain things that go against my values, like modesty, I'll take a stand on. It's important to have *hayaa* – it's quite sacred itself. A lot of parents don't want sex education. I think you can have it, however, you don't want them to feel it's all ok to go do anything.

(Husna)

I did speak to her ... she was very calm. I felt awkward. I told her what she needed to know at the time. Even now, I know they do a lot more, I said you can ask me, so you don't look things up in the internet ... things will come up that you shouldn't see. I have to prompt it and then we have a discussion. I don't know how much else she knows, girls talk, teachers talk ... but as a Muslim, she needs to know *hayaa* in front of family on these matters.

(Nilofer)

There's a huge issue when kids in the playground talk about it. Every child is different. Some aren't interested in this at all. It was easy with the first – he was really easy – to talk about puberty issues. He got education about this from madrassah and I topped it up. He didn't watch the video, he wasn't too interested in the leaflet either.

(Dina)

While these observations relate to the values of *hayaa* in the context of SRE, other parts of the mothers' interviews made passing mention of the need for modesty in relation to changing facilities for PE and swimming. One mother, reflecting on her own schooling in an English northern town, noted that 'having Christian values through my schooling was compatible with family values in those days. It was the same moral lines me and my Christian friends had' (Asiya, business management, L5). While sharing their experiences, these mothers repeated the same need to have clearer information early on, so they could understand what was part of the curriculum, what was not and what the contents of any visual material would be. Had there been time in the interviews and focus groups, the importance of SRE in relation to safeguarding issues would certainly have been discussed, judging from the amount of concern the mothers expressed about SRE.

Securitizing school

Another challenge was the culture of surveillance in schools. Just over a fifth of my participants expressed their concern about the way the Preventing Violent Extremism (PVE) strategy affects their children in school. Mothers not only raised the issue when listing the challenges they face, some also mentioned it as part of the discourse about the media and Muslims, while others – particularly those working in schools – named it as an example of the ways their professional role, personal faith and parental role coincided to affect their communication with the school.

The Prevent strategy is part of the UK's counter-terrorism legislation. Soon after the London bombings in 2005 (known as 7/7), the government reviewed its existing terrorism legislation and devised a counter-terrorism strategy, Contest, 'a multi-dimensional strategy corresponding to the multi-faceted nature of terrorism' (Choudhury and Fenwick, 2011: 13). Contest has four main strands: Pursue, Prepare, Protect and a fourth 'Prevent'. The ideas behind Prevent are stated in official policy documentation:

> Our objectives for the revised Prevent strategy will be to: respond to the ideological challenge of terrorism and the threat we face from those who promote it, prevent people from being drawn into terrorism and ensure that they are given appropriate advice and support and work with a wide range of sectors (including in particular education, faith, health, the internet and criminal justice) where there are risks of radicalisation which we need to address.
>
> (Home Office, 2011: 63)

On the ground, the programme is designed to prevent people, including young people and children, being drawn into terrorism and radicalization through non-violent extremist ideas, in addition to the original mandate of preventing violent extremism.

In 2007, as part of the Prevent policy, the Channel programme was introduced, to which young people, particularly school students, could be referred if education or youth work professionals saw evidence of a certain 'indicator'. The multi-agency Channel programme consists of police, schools, health providers and local authority representatives. The 22 indicators range from 'engagement with a group' to 'the intent to cause harm' and finally 'the capability to cause harm'. Other 'engagement' indicators are:

- feelings of grievance and injustice
- feeling under threat
- a need for identity, meaning and belonging
- a desire for status
- a desire for excitement and adventure
- a need to dominate and control others
- susceptibility to indoctrination
- a desire for political or moral change (Webber, 2016: 2).

The Counter-Terrorism and Security (CTS) Act was passed in 2015. This extended the impact the Prevent programme went on to have in public institutions. The CTS Act placed responsibilities on professionals in the public sector to refer potential services users – be they patients in a doctor's surgery or children as young as 4 – if they are deemed to be at risk or vulnerable to being radicalized.

Analysis of the Prevent programme (Khan, 2009) and the CTS Bill has raised concerns lest they impinge on children's human rights. The Institute of Race Relations' report – *Prevent and the Children's Right's Convention* (Webber, 2016) – presents a detailed evaluation of the effects of the Prevent programme's aims in relation to upholding specific Articles in the Convention on the Rights of the Child, such as protecting 'children's freedom of thought, conscience and religion, subject to limitations prescribed by the law and necessary to protect public safety, order, health or morals, or the fundamental rights and freedoms of others' Article 14 (Webber, 2016: 3). The report concludes:

> All the indications are that the strategy is undermining professional standards, educational independence, children's rights to freedom of thought, expression and association and principles of non-discrimination, and is alienating Muslim young people and communities.
>
> (Webber, 2016: 13)

Intersecting the trajectory of PVE legislation is the ongoing discussion and policy iterations related to 'community cohesion'. The seeds of contemporary community cohesion discourse are found in the aftermath of the damaging riots between Pakistani and English youth in the northern towns of England in 2001. Issues such as housing and labour market penalties have been cited in a number of studies to explain why these uprisings occurred. Several scholars have offered detailed analyses of the disturbances; it suffices here that public discourse around integration, citizenship, immigration and community cohesion gained traction (Cantle, 2001).

Citizenship and community cohesion aspects of the National Curriculum underwent significant changes too. Even when policies tried to separate the counter-terrorism strategy from the integration and cohesion agenda, the fact that they overlap cannot be ignored. The requirement to infuse 'fundamental British values' into the school curriculum, for example, is directly related to a review of the Prevent strategy (Bolleton and Richardson, 2015). Each of these subjects is under scrutiny and development in both academia and the UK press. However the relationship between securitization, education and the teaching of morals and values is perceived, one fact remains constant, though: for the average parent these discourses are remote or incomprehensible. These are complex, multidimensional subjects that have an impact on the daily lives of all children in school. At the same time they are are equally esoteric in terms of parents' understanding of them.

In the ethos of reflexive research, I acknowledge the effect of timing and location as relevant to understanding the mothers' responses. At the time of interviewing, the CTS Bill was being widely discussed in mainstream media and questioned by civil rights groups such as Liberty and the National Association of Head Teachers (NAHT). The Bill proposed making it a legal duty for prisons, the NHS, local authorities as well as schools to detect those vulnerable to extremism and refer them to the Channel programme. Questions raised concerned the extent to which teachers and childminders make serious mistakes when they refer children as young as 5 on suspicion of them being radicalized. The Act was passed in July 2015, soon after I had conducted the majority of the interviews. Subsequently, a steady stream of news articles and commentary highlighted cases where school staff raised concerns over children as young as 3, adding to a 'surge in referrals' which has seen '400 children under the age of 10 ... referred for deradicalisation in the last four years' (Busby, 2016).

It is significant that the mothers who spoke at length about their concerns were involved in the education system, either as a staff member or as a school governor. Their professional role afforded them even greater knowledge about the Act than the other mothers in my study. The following mother's narrative shows the splintered ways safeguarding, surveillance, identity and agency affect one another, intertwined in a way that our discussion captures:

> In terms of challenges I face, with the CTS Bill going on ...
> it's approaching the school – knowing when it's appropriate

to approach the school. The focus of everything has changed. It's so difficult though sometimes. For example, when we're driving around locally, to school or somewhere, she reads those newspaper boards with the headlines saying 'Muslim terrorist' and asks me why it says that. As a mum I have to answer using simple 'good' and 'bad' people terms. I try not to make her feel negative, but it's everywhere. Since the CTS Bill, I'm worried about what she hears on the news and if it goes to school the wrong way, so at home, I've blocked the news in the living room, no BBC, SKY ... nothing.

SD: What effect does all this have on your relationship with her school?

N: It makes the necessity to be involved more than ever before. Making sure we're not misunderstood. We need to integrate more into the system, do more when events are being organized, go into the classroom, reading, meeting other mums. I can understand why some mums don't make an effort and can't be bothered. They're not confident sometimes, or feel inadequate, some have language barriers.

Now that I know what's involved in the PVE training, I know that 'modest clothing', for example, is part of detecting radicalization. So what do I do? I would like my daughter to change separately, for her own childhood innocence's sake. Every year, I've spoken or written to the teacher about it and it's fine, she can change on her own, if the girls and boys aren't separated. But this year, do I ask the new teacher who's just out of training? Will she take this to mean I'm radicalizing my daughter? What do I do?

(Nasra)

For Nasra, detailed awareness of the legislation and of anecdotes about children who had been questioned made her sensitive about the impact of surveillance on herself and her daughter. The frustration she felt over what can be discussed with a class teacher came through from the way she weighed decisions regarding changing facilities and clothes.

Mothers of older children, further into their secondary school education and at college took a similar line to Nasra, saying they felt fearful and were specifically concerned about social media online. They worried about problems associated with the fast flow of information, the intangible sources and what they believed was their parental responsibility to manage potential undesirable influences:

> Tahira: I must admit, I did worry, as things have changed so much. Like with my son going to college. The thing is, you are exposed to a lot more, you worry about are they naive? It's an age that they're curious.
>
> SD: Do you worry about this as a parent?
>
> T: You do worry about this, a slight worry. You hear of kids from decent families going to do silly things. You do feel with social media, and the older they get, you don't know who their friends are, like the old-fashioned way. You think you know your children, but it gets harder when they are older. As a parent you feel cut out. It's a very different world, the influences are not just the home. You worry about their influences and what they're taking in. You wonder about their maturity. Sometimes they want to wind you up by joking ... but then you think are you joking. Young boys think they know it all. I find it's a boy attitude.
>
> (Tahira)

> Zainab: We have to deal with these programmes (*Jihadi Brides*, BBC) they show now. Her friends asked if she's watched them. I watched it with my teenage daughter. She was shocked and said 'how could they do this?' We know Islamically this isn't right. No way it's right to do this ... it's not. On what basis are they doing this ... what is going on? As parents, we have to handle it, how these programmes and things affect our kids ... and I feel sorry for the kids now. They are going through *a lot* more than what we are going through. One thing's their age, and how they are being seen by others. They have to put a lot more effort in, to make others understand what Islam is. We never had such a pressurized thing.
>
> (Zainab)

Mothers who work in the education sector had insights as both a parent and a professional. These shaped their concerns about surveillance in school and what was said about it. As a member of staff at a state school that serves predominantly working-class families, Parveen encountered colleagues who made generalized remarks during training sessions on preventing radicalization about the mosque being a site of abuse. On the other hand, a few of Parveen's colleagues found the training inappropriate: 'Staff were coming up to me later and saying they didn't agree with it. They didn't get it ... and they were quietly saying "what is this?" to me.'

> Afreen: All this extremism, it's so scary. Both [teenage children] were on Facebook – and the things that were coming through, groups coming through, generic invitations to conferences, but you don't know what type of conference. They both came to me and were both talking about it. It's all quite scary and you think: where, how? How did this happen – I don't want to be one of those parents one day.
>
> SD: What is it that scares you?
>
> A: Because they're exposed to so much now. Whereas before I could monitor that. I thought I knew what's going on. Now there's anything or everything. It's sometimes at night, you can't sleep, you think, what if somebody ... you don't know who these people are with extremist views? Now I have a ten o'clock curfew on iPads/phones and computers, they might think mum is too protective. It's so hard.
>
> Even with younger kids, at work, we've had to report children because of the criteria – it's something ridiculous. I had to report it, I said it was ridiculous ... and they saw the same – it didn't make sense. As a Muslim teacher, I'm under pressure. A non-Muslim teacher could see it didn't make sense and not report it – but I have to.
>
> (Afreen)

A great many emotions were evident in the discussions and interviews. Efforts to manage and safeguard children while feeling hurt about the profiling and being misunderstood, create a new state of being, raising new questions for all to whom the welfare of children, of citizens and national security are important. At the same time, inclusion, plurality and the rights and responsibilities of citizenship are central principles that are part of our daily lives and which cannot be ignored. The women's expressions of concern fit Gillies' (2006) definition of parents' emotional capital as 'emotional investments made by parents as part of their desire to promote their children's wellbeing and prospects' (2006: 286). Gillies recognizes the efforts and anxieties that consume parents and observes that the emotional investments of working-class mothers' relationship to school 'may be directed towards day to day survival at school as well as maximizing formal educational opportunities'. Applying this insight to the mothers' remarks reveals their fundamental aim to safeguard their children's very existence, on terms equal to the protection of other children. To these women, survival means not being viewed through a criminal lens, not being questioned by social workers about exactly how their children have been raised and not being placed on an allusive 'list' which is itself becoming something of an urban legend – mothers discuss 'the list' with mounting concern.

Reading between the lines of the data elicits wider implications. Sometimes silences in the interview, disjointed narratives, changing tack of their own accord, revealed that a participant felt challenged by the implications of surveillance. Some mothers said more than others about choosing a school, describing the ways they went about avoiding those they felt their child might not be comfortable in, where they might be racially hampered or generally unaccepted. We saw in Chapter 5 that some went to great lengths to make sure the 'feel' of the school was right for their child. However, with the Prevent duty prompting all teachers in all schools to survey pupils and by extension their parents, the very attitudes and feelings they had tried to avoid are now inescapable. They found it difficult to accept the surveillance framework that situates both them and their children as threats to UK security. Collectively, they voiced frustration. At the time of interviewing, my own children were in various stages of full-time education so I had similar feelings on various levels. I had a delicate task keeping these concerns out of our interviews.

This chapter has brought together three areas, criss-crossed by several minor themes, to build up a picture of how the mothers' positions in relation to their children's schools shift according to how they need to react to and interact with the situations they face. They show both agency and detachment; confidence and confusion. Chapter 7 continues to seek answers for what the mothers themselves have identified as areas they want to improve in home–school relations.

Chapter 7

Narrative bridges

As a parent and professional I can see the problem: teachers need to be aware of the lifestyles and cultures that affect engagement or disengagement. There's a difference between religion and home culture.

(Rizwana)

It's about humanity, we need to give respect to each other. If we started with educating the parents a lot of it would be fine.

(Erum)

It's very important for children to a get a solid education. Education is the base of living … it's anything that helps you help other people and you'll get rewarded for that.

(Hafsa)

It's necessary to be involved more than ever before, making sure we're not misunderstood.

(Nasra)

In the Preface I stressed the need to hear from those who are silent, that their presence is required, that their voices be heard, that they themselves construct a bridge with their narratives. In their distinctive ways, the mothers in this study have shared their experiences and challenges educating their children in state schools. They have carved their own narratives instead of accepting prefabricated stories, and articulated their experiences to fill crevices and shape their numerous realities. Their voices have directed the contents of this book.

This chapter has two purposes. The first is to present an unanticipated subject that arose in several interviews and emerged in all the focus groups: mosque/madrassah education. The second is to explore the mothers' responses to my closing question during the interviews and discussions: could they suggest any ways to encourage better communication and understanding between the home and school?

Regarding and re-guarding capital

In the study, 'education' was understood in the broadest sense and included spiritual, moral and academic grounding (see Chapter 4). From a mothers' perspective, talking about her child's education included their attending supplementary schooling in the shape of a mosque class or madrassah, although this is not the only form of supplementary faith education. Faith education was discussed at length in the two focus groups, and references made to it in a quarter of the individual interviews. Whether it was delivered in a mosque, community hall or someone's home, mothers described it as an integral part of their child's life. The larger focus group discussed the frequency of lessons and their commitment as parents to making sure their children attended the classes – while ensuring they were not overloaded with studies.

In the smaller group discussion mothers probed and debated their views on prioritizing supplementary classes over other extra-curricular activities and school commitments. An example was given of a school trip being shortened because half the pupils had an after-school madrassah class. Opinions voiced included the concern that daily faith classes could be too frequent and how parents needed to be better organized about managing children's madrassah and after-school commitments. The mothers reached a consensus that 'when it's a one-off issue', such as the school trip, madrassahs should accommodate educational trips that benefit the children. Whether better community links are needed between schools and local madrassahs in some localities is a matter for further research. The group discussed how several mothers strove to balance their children's out-of-school duties and the school day. Some alluded to the contrast in the ethos children encounter in their two sites of learning and the challenges inherent in the differing *ways* of learning.

Pedagogical differences certainly do exist between traditional mosque education and mainstream schooling. However, the landscape of supplementary education in the UK is changing. Supplementary mosque or madrassah education varies hugely from one Muslim community to another, depending on location, socio-economic factors, how long the community has been established, what type of cultural heritage they bring with them, the mosque committees' education levels and so forth. Even in one geographical area, there may be several contrasting types of provision, just as one would find variety among Sunday schools between different church denominations. The traditional style of rote learning Qur'anic Arabic, continues to be the customary way the language is taught in mosque classes. The purpose, initially, is to enable children to read the sacred text phonetically until they acquire fluency in reading the script. For those who want to take their reading to a higher level (usually by their teens), the science of recitation also involves attention to the intricate tempo, intonation and rhythm and training the vocal chords. For the majority, memorizing the set passages and reading the entire Qur'an from cover to cover is akin to a 'rite of passage', celebrated in various ways determined by the family's cultural heritage. The teaching methods are not necessarily static. With developments in teacher training, madrassah management and policy creation and more UK-educated teachers managing these classes, a change is slowly taking place. It still has a way to go until more qualified staff join the sector, however (Faith Associates, 2016).

Curriculum, syllabus and safeguarding requirements have also been developed with training and standard setting becoming the norm. A madrassah manager from the South East discussed their specific requirements: 'We make sure all our teachers are CRB cleared and they have to have read the policies and sign a contract to abide by them. We have safeguarding training they go on.' While these developments have reached some localities sooner than others, the negative stereotype persists, as Parveen's narrative illustrates:

> Work colleagues hate the fact that kids go off to mosque. I've never heard anyone say anything nice ... they think they're being radicalized and can't do their homework. Everyone uses the word 'radicalization' as we've had that training – so they're all experts now. Some children come up to me and say what they've learnt and I praise it like any other achievement.

> (Parveen)

Parveen's colleagues' reaction to the mosque classes could reflect the negativity associated with media news stories about mosques. Or it could be opinions about race and class and about what is seen as an acceptable extracurricular activity. In the UK, as in parts of Europe and the US, it is not uncommon to have faith weekend schools, language classes and a host of other children's culture building activities, particularly for migrant groups. How madrassah education fits into the discourse on inclusion is another potential area to explore.

There are subtle differences in parents' efforts to supplement their children's education. The extra-curricular activities and tuition referred to by Reay, in her case studies on social reproduction of middle- and working-class mothers (1998; 2000), for example, reveals the ways mothers from different social classes approach involvement with their children's education. The studies show that the 'social, cultural and material advantages' that affect educational success, are the stock of the middle classes. Reay's arguments about social injustice and inequality, confirmed by the mothers' narratives in her study, show how inequitable 'success' can be.

A class variable regarding madrassah attendance/supplementary schooling is less prominent in the narratives of the women in my study. Instead, the mothers clearly enact the workings of 'social and cultural reproduction' (Crozier and Reay, 2005), assuming the responsibility for making sure the spiritual and operational aspects of faith are managed in their children's lives. The aspirational and better resourced mothers showed greater prowess in choosing which type of class their child will attend. Several bought in home tutors' services and were discerning about the type of classes, teachers and timings. The less-resourced mothers, on the other hand, sent their children to their nearest madrassah classes. In terms of capital, the choice of supplementary schooling is part of the repertoire of Muslim parents' investment in their children and is relevant to the wider discussion of capital later in this chapter.

Improving communication

Participants interpreted the question about communication in different ways. Most spoke about what they believed would improve communication between the home and the school; others returned to the subject of identity and how to clarify misconceptions. A few took an introspective view of barriers from within the community and outlined the need for community groups and individuals to be proactive in forging links and participating in school life. Mothers who had worked in the education and social services sectors broadened their responses to include the role of multiple agency relationships if there are signs of parents not cooperating with schools. Drawing on their experience, this is their reading of improving communication:

> It's a combination of factors, schools do look out for them and in all fairness they give them designated prayer areas in Ramadan and schools are trying and the parents don't know how the teachers bend over and change things to help them. As a parent and professional I can see the problem: teachers need to be aware of the lifestyles and cultures that affect engagement or disengagement – as it's complicated. There's a difference between religion and home culture.

Lots of things need to be done with some Muslim parents. Some don't get it ... like parents' evening, safeguarding issues, lots of thing are messed up because of culture; there's domestic issues, fathers in prison – the works, that's lifestyles.

Teachers are in a unique position to identify if a child's not achieving, sometimes more than the parents or carers and looking at the family set-up and social side ... just like other communities.

(Rizwana)

In a similar vein, Mouna, a mother whose professional role involves supporting marginalized women and families, observed:

Both the community and the school need to be more open about what they don't understand. The media is not the true story. Schools and agencies need to understand where the parents are coming from and give positive support. If there are problems, then working with the parent and the child together, like we have with mothers and daughters, can build better relationships.

(Mouna, company director, L1)

Back to identities

A prevalent response, given by most of the mothers, returned to correcting essentialized identities. The mothers stressed the need to be seen and understood without being labelled according to preconceived ideas, articulating 'the problematic aspect of identity politics ... the politics of recognition' (Vincent, 2000: 6). The fact that this subject was raised again shows the strength of feeling about identity construction, about resistance, about the authentic voice. As in real life, these narratives have no neat, linear progression; they flit from one issue to another, loosely strung as one area of life touches another. The result, as the following extracts show, is a mix of being introspective and critical, retrospective and hopeful. We see evolving identities, oscillating between the public image of a group and the private lived experience of being an individual, a parent and 'just a mum', as one participant remarked. The mothers felt a negative public image precedes their relationship with school. Even those mothers with no professional connection to education or community sectors are vocal about challenging stereotypes and misconceptions:

They need to hear the views so all kids are comfortable ... some of them have wrong views ... on both sides. It could be our kids with wrong views 'cos of the wars in other places in the world.

My own school RE was go *gudwara*, go mosque, this is a church, that's how they pray ... and that's it – that's RE. Nowadays, it's more intense as there's so much more that happens. I know when kids see, and don't know you, they'll come out with things they've been fed with from home. But when they know, then they can see 'he's just the same as us, they're not a terrorist or shoe bomber'.

(Sonia)

Actually that's quite difficult to think of advice, as there are Muslims and there are 'Muslims'. To one Muslim, it may mean a completely different need and demands and others might be no different to anyone else. So, I suppose the awareness that Muslims are very different and not to make assumptions. Listen to what the parents are saying. One thing I've learnt is you can't make assumptions. As a parent, do not assume teacher will know anything about Muslims. You literally have to spell it out. Would a trainee teacher know these things ... are we leaving it up to them to know?

(Tahira)

I think some education on Islam and myths, giving the fact about things when training teachers. There's a lot of difference between Muslims. When I was pregnant and talked to my class about the baby etc., some parents came in and said they don't like their child learning all this as it's not discussed in their culture. Now they're also Pakistani parents and Muslim like me, but have a different perspective. I explained it to them as part of nature and life cycles and part of what I was teaching the children. So there is a lot of difference.

(Afreen)

Sometimes I think people create problems from the outside and those come into schools, and make trouble for everyone. It's better to have respect for everyone. We need respect in this way and give respect that way.

(Kausar)

One member of staff likes to organize socials around betting, or drinking is a big part – that's the two things I just won't do. When they try to be inclusive, they suggest going to an Indian restaurant.

I've tried explaining ... but it's that 'just do a bit, it's harmless, I won't tell anyone' comments that show they don't get it.

(Afreen)

I think I'd say have good communication with parents as many parents, especially if they come from outside, don't know anything. And don't assume we are all bad.

(Fahmida)

We need more interfaith dialogue between parents and school; in some areas communities are quite polarized.

(Catherine)

I would advise more basic knowledge is necessary to combat misrepresentation and myths about our community.

(Hibaaq)

... we have to do actions to change the environment. I'm a person, I just want them to see that. I don't want them to judge me on my hijab and *jilbab*. At first they thought I was quiet, but when I spoke they were shocked and their whole body language changed ... then afterwards they see past that [the clothes]. I don't judge them, so I don't want them to judge me. It's about humanity, we need to give respect to each other. If we started with educating the parents a lot of it would be fine.

(Erum)

* * *

Zarah: Ideally they need people from the community in the schools ... but with Muslims it is difficult, as we have different cultures. But still, I think they need some training, maybe someone who explains what is Muslim, why they celebrate Eid, why they fast, why they pray.

SD: After 21 years in the education system, you still feel there's a need for training?

Z: Yes. Sometimes even though you talk, they don't listen, or forget, they need to hear it again. Eighty per cent in the school I'm in are Muslims – staff understand a lot more because 6–7 staff are

Muslim. But you know because of the media, it is very difficult. We don't have strong Muslim community here, there are not people who come to represent.

The media is saying Islam is intolerant. Every day in the staff room they bring the METRO in and the first page is someone did something. When the staff read this, the only thing they think is it's not a good religion. Even though they know us as staff, as good, but they get bombarded with the negative. Even for us as Muslim, what can we say? They never ask directly, but you can see in their eyes and I volunteer and say 'this is not Islam'. When they have questions, I will go and explain, it's part of my 'job'.

(Zarah, parent advisor, L3)

Zarah's periodic struggle in the staffroom cuts across faith, ethnicity and class, as she alludes further to a local community that cannot represent itself adequately. Her extract exemplifies the damage negative headlines have on parents' daily interactions with school, a theme identified in Chapter 5. The other mothers articulated wide-ranging suggestions about what they felt would help home–school relations. These had one common thread: better information for teachers that differentiates between faith and culture.

So many of the mothers placed identity at the centre of their responses about improving home–school relationships that it perhaps creates a new perspective on who they are and how their role vis-à-vis their child's education has evolved. I offer the description of an 'authenticating mother', to sign-post their contemporary position. The struggle to authenticate their existence and identity on a daily basis recurred throughout the group discussions. In particular, their language in the interviews included that of validating, of proving and justifying in overt and subtle ways, where they stand. Throughout this book, we have seen the way the mothers evaluate their position, bringing to the fore their roots, their contemporary lives and by extension their agency. In *Maternal Thinking* Ruddick comments on the evolving nature of mothers' voices in the 1980s. It still rings true today:

Maternal voices have been drowned by professional theory, ideologies of motherhood, sexist arrogance, and childhood fantasy. Voices that have been distorted and censored can only be *developing* voices. Alternately silenced and edging towards speech, mothers' voices are not voices of mothers as they are, but as they are becoming. As mothers struggle towards responsible thinking, they will transform the thought they are beginning to articulate and the knowledge they are determined to share.

(Ruddick, 1989: 40)

How these women situate themselves is relevant beyond the school gates. The way the mothers in my study identify themselves is useful to those working across the public service sectors, particularly – as Williams (2015) asserts – where families are involved:

Spaces are needed in which parenting narrative is valued, particularly for under-represented groups to inform the development of culturally competent and relevant family well being early interventions, while simultaneously encouraging client self-efficacy.

(Williams, 2015: 2)

The aforementioned final comments – intersectional, contradictory, exploratory and explanatory – offer insight into the intricate position of Muslim mothers in relation to their children's education and general upbringing.

Communication and behaviour

Some mothers responded to the question about communication by talking specifically about their children's behaviour. In one of the focus group sites, long-term behaviour issues was a priority, particularly as the mothers there had larger families and therefore a broader experience of behaviour. Their narratives were influenced by what had happened with their older children who had left school, and the challenges experienced at a community level. As one mother said: 'when there are behaviour issues and then when kids end up in the streets ... and these behaviour problems are muted in the beginning and we don't know. They'll wait for parents' evening and then it's too late ... so communicating earlier would be better.' This corroborated Zarah's views, who was from the same community. Zarah described a memory from the early days of her professional work in the late 1990s, when children coming from Somalia were settling into schools in London – and how some parents and schools moved forward as a community:

Two boys I remember, one found it difficult to sit in the classroom, disruptive. The whole day they'd sit outside the classroom. I talked to the parents, and they said he had hole in the bottom of his back from an injury. The children came and didn't know they have to sit, there was no system they were coming from, like being in a classroom and listening quietly. Also he had a physical problem … then I explained to the headteacher and she understood. We supported the child and worked with him and he improved. So then, from there, I found Somali parents need to understand the education system. I planned coffee mornings and asked teachers to come and talk about behaviour policy, homework policy, how to support children with homework (like reading stories in Somali). I started like this. Then we used to hire halls and invite primary and secondary schools parents and talked about how to support children. They would call each other and come – just mothers.

Next we included fathers also. They usually had a hundred excuses, some think they know everything. In the end they knew they needed to support everything. You see the mums understood – but we wanted the men to understand, some did listen. In the first school I worked in I ran Parents: Partners in Learning and I was covering basic things like supporting children with English, just taking them to the library; fill in forms; ask questions about stories in your language, help with reading and grammar; showing them how to use websites.

If there is one thing these women were united about, it was the value they placed on educating their children. This book has shown the concern mothers have for their children's education: the ways they have supported it, the positive relationships they build with schools and the challenges they face. Conceptually, the narratives I have shared are relevant to Yosso's discussion on 'community cultural wealth' (2005), which asks: '*Whose culture has capital?*' Yosso focuses on the practical manifestation of how schools under-utilize the cultural wealth children from minorities possess. Utilizing such cultural capital is a way to do something for real inclusion, a nexus that can bring parents together on subjects that go beyond the outdated 'saree, steel band and samosa' tropes of diversity. Broader themes such as the environment, arts and culture, science and maths, literature – all of which are central to the school curriculum and particularly to global citizenship – present opportunities for meaningful cultural exchange.

International food stalls have become a feature of summer fetes, opening the way for more parental involvement. Similarly themed events – on arts and crafts from around the world, for example – could include a broad range of disciplines. Schools with eco-friendly projects can use them to draw in parents for whom academic-related support is daunting, as hands-on activities are an effective way to bring parents together to support the school's projects. I have seen successful projects in primary schools that blended faith and culture in a way that made all the parents and children feel included on occasions like Eid, when international fashion, arts and food were given equal importance and parents from ten or more different cultural backgrounds shared aspects of their heritage.

Retrospective, introspective: perspective

I started with an intersectional framework and I end with it. This book does not take a single problem and offer a neatly aligned solution to it. It has raised the curtain on a small group of women from the largest faith minority and sizeable ethnic minorities in the UK, and shared their experiences. Where normally gender, class and race intersect in ways that show marginalization, the axis the mothers constructed places their faith identity firmly at the centre of their experience. Thanks to the ways Muslims have been placed in the public imagination by the media and political discourse, the struggles they talk of at times position the faith element above gender, race or class. Their accounts of how they view education, what their experiences have been, what they find challenging, what they do not understand, how they contribute, why they do or do not engage, have filled some of the spaces between assumptions, conjecture and fact.

Schools and parents need there to be dialogue between them: that much is uncontested. For the interests of the children, for genuine education that moves society in the direction of compassion and understanding, we need dialogue. More so when there is a dearth of communication and an excess of half-truths and misinformation.

As I began this book acknowledging the personal, it seems right to end with a mother's narrative, told in free-association style, that sets aside the mother–child–home–school rubric so we can hear what she wanted to say. I hope the following vignette – a combination of my field notes and our interaction – brings the diverse subjects in this book back to the heart of the matter: that mothers' commitment to education is heard and their passionate words utilized as the material to build long-lasting bridges with schools. Acknowledging the power of personal stories, Michael Apple expounds their relevance for educators thus:

> Much of the impetus behind personal stories is moral. Education correctly is seen as an ethical enterprise. The personal is seen as a way to re-awaken ethical and aesthetic sensitivities that increasingly have been purged from the scientific discourse of

too many educators. Or it is seen as a way of giving a voice to the subjectivities of people who have been silenced. There is much to commend in this position. Indeed any approach that, say, evacuates the aesthetic, the personal, and the ethical from our activities as educators, is not about education at all. It is about training.

(Apple, 2005: 71)

I leave you with Amaal.

June 2015

For a second week we have the use of the community room and I await Amaal's arrival. A ten-minute delay and I reflect on how this hardly matters in the grand scheme of life and locations I've visited, to talk to mothers. My thoughts stray to the 'to do' list I drew up the night before to tick my own family, correspondence and work boxes, to ensure I was out the of the house by 7a.m., with all bases covered for the next twelve hours until I returned. If only Amaal knew ... but she'll see me differently. I wonder what she must have to rig to meet me this morning and just then, she arrives, a little breathless, having rushed to our room through the warren of corridors to reach this side of the school.

A: She was sleeping. I've just got her up. Sorry, I hope you don't mind. I'm looking after my sister's daughter as she's doing a shift now ... she leaves her with me. I didn't realize she was doing today. Is it ok?

Once she's reassured her niece's presence is not a problem, she sighs with relief, just long enough to catch a stray thought: she apologizes again, anticipating she might have to leave early if the 3-year-old makes a fuss. With the infant sprawled across her chest, we start to chat about the morning rush of getting children out to school. 'How about when you were at school Amaal, what was it like?' Not a question I planned to ask but a natural way in, I felt, to focus on her 'self'. And she was eager, on this summer morning sat in West London at 9.45a.m., to take us both back to Somalia. Her narrative unravelled.

A: My father had a good government job, we were comfortable and I went to school where I had cousins and sisters ... lots of family. You know it's big families there. So we were all in school, and then I had to come here to the UK because of the situation there. With the war, it was getting worse, girls were getting raped, there was violence, my parents wanted me to continue my education outside and I was one of the eldest too.

So with my father's job ... he knew people, they sent me to an aunt here in London, I was only 17. My father was afraid of me changing, but my mother wasn't – she trusted me and I've kept my promise to her. She said 'I trust my daughter, I'm sending her for education'.

Amaal adjusts her niece's position as she's fallen asleep and continues.

A: And I promised to my mother, I wasn't going to change, and I would get my education. *She places her hand on her stomach, in the same way people place their hand on their heart; it is no coincidence the words for 'mercy' and 'womb' come from the same root in her mother tongue – Arabic.* I promised her I would do that, she could trust me. So here I went to college to English classes first and I wanted to carry on but after two years, I got married. I was missing my family and I needed some security. My in-laws were good to me. I had my first child when I was young, and my mother-in-law helped me ... and I started to work, she looked after my baby when I was working. At the same time it got worse in Somalia so my brothers and sisters had to leave too, they were getting older. Some of them went to Pakistan and studied there. It was my priority to send them help so I worked as a cleaner in the airport. I sent them help by working. At the same time I had another child, then after a long gap I had one more son. It was very difficult, especially the gap ... and I wanted my eldest to do well, and she's, thank God graduated now, looking for Masters courses ... but I don't know yet which one.

SD: How did you manage?

A: It was tough, my mother-in-law helped me. After she died, then a sister came, they helped too like with the children and taking care of the flat, and helping with the brothers and sisters that came here for their education. Out of all of us, three have passed away.

SD: So what did they do at university?

A: From the ten left, there's now a pharmacist, a dentist, two working in IT, two did biomedical, one is doing post-grad at Oxford – *the* Oxford. The youngest is doing his engineering degree, he's given me a hard time, changing courses twice.

SD: And what happened to your education, Amaal?

A: Huh! My mother sent me here for education! But I'm not anything – my brain's not working. I did pass Level 1 English but I still have to do an Access course as I want to be a nurse – I want to help people. I want to be a mother who is educated and can educate others. But it's the home, cooking, jobs, working and working, or running around with the children I couldn't do much study. I'm doing some care work now, but not enough hours.

… I want to study now. I'm going to go to college, and do the foundation health care. I've got two sons still in primary, so I have to look there as well. I don't know … with Somali families, the mothers can manage them 'til 15, then they lose control, especially of the boys. Sometimes it's the father's fault – not being around enough. You know, it's some mothers' fault too. They bring their sons up like kings. These men go to work, come back and act like they're holding the sun and sky up for you. That's their attitude … they sleep and don't think the family is their job. So of course the mothers are frustrated. But then people shouldn't raise their sons like that, should they?

Amaal brings her narrative to a close and looks at me expectantly; awaiting the start of the formal interview. I open my notebook and stare at the naivety of my questions in relation to her gendered, classed, raced, migrant's account moulded around her commitment to education. If this doesn't say something, there's nothing in my notebook that will.

The participants

Pseudonym	Ethnicity	Education level	Work	No of children
Location 1 (L1)				
Husna	BD	Degree	Project officer	3
Sonia	PK	FE/GNVQ	Admin	2
Mouna	BD	Postgraduate	Director	4
Rehana	PK	Degree	Officer	3
Shama	BD	School	Care assistant	4
Adel	Arab	School		1
Maha	Kurdish	Middle school		1
Location 2 (L2)				
Erum	PK	FE	Admin	3
Saira	PK	FE	Qur'an teacher	3
Naila	BD	FE/YTS*	Childcare	4
Focus Group participants				
A	BD	School	School Support	3
B	BD	School		4
C	BD	School		2
D	BD	School	Admin Assistant	3
E	BD	FE	Part-time	4
F	BD	School		2
G	BD	School		4
H	BD	FE	School support	5
I	BD	School		3
J	BD	School		3
L	BD	School		4
Location 3 (L3)				
Huma	BD	School	Retail	4
Zarah	Somali	Degree	Parent advisor	3

Rizwana	PK	A-levels	Learning Support Assistant	3
Amaal	Somali	FE	Care Assistant	3
Hodan	Somali	School	Part-time carer services	4
Fatima	Somali	School		5
Hafsa	Somali	FE	Part-time	3
Hibaaq	Somali	School		4
Aisha	Somali	School		3
Location 4 (L4)				
Tahira	IND	Degree	Education/ activist	5
Amira	PK	Degree	Solicitor	4
Mariam	PK	FE	School admin	4
Huda	PK	FE	Student	2
Location 5 (L5)				
Bushra	PK	Degree	Postgraduate student	6
Afreen	PK	Postgrad	Deputy head	3
Wahida	PK/IND	Degree	Medical health professional	4
Nasra	Arab	Postgrad	Teacher	2
Parveen	BD	Degree	Learning support assistant	2
Saba	PK	Degree	Counsellor	4
Nilofer	BD	Degree	Teacher	2
Asma	PK	HE	Learning support assistant	3
Jameela	PK	Postgrad	Postgraduate student	4
Catherine	En	Degree	Teacher	1
Asiyah	PK	Degree	Corporate management	3
Zainab	IND	Degree	Medical health professional	4
Fahmida	PK	School		3

Kausar	PK	School	English as a Second Language student	4
Dina	PK	School	Learning support assistant/ mosque teacher	4
Summayyah	PK	Postgrad	Qur'an teacher	3
Emma	England	Degree	Medical health professional	2
Muslim Mamas				
Latifa	BD	Degree	Teacher/ Education centre manager	3
Razia	BD	Degree	Social services/ Education	2

Notes
YTS: Youth Training Schemes
FE: Further education, post-16
L3: Fewer work and biographical details were obtained for this focus group.
A space in the 'work' column denotes that the participant was not in any paid work.

Glossary

Ayah	A sign, a miracle and the common name for a verse of the Qur'an.
Aqiqah	The celebration to mark the birth of a baby by sacrificing a sheep and feeding people, particularly those in need.
Eid	Two festivals of celebration. The first, Eid-ul-Fitr marks the end of the fasts in Ramadan. The second, Eid-ul-Adha is the celebration of sacrifice at the end of the Hajj pilgrimage.
Hadith (plural: *ahadith*)	The second source of Islamic sacred text: the hadith are the sayings and observations of the Prophet Muhammad (peace be upon him).
Hajj	The annual pilgrimage to The Sacred Mosque in Mecca and surrounding areas. It is obligatory once in a person's lifetime if they have the means and good health to do so.
Halal	What is lawful and permissible.
Hayaa	Modesty, self-respect.
Hijab	A head scarf covering the hair and neck.
Madrassa	An educational institution.
Qur'an	The revelation to Prophet Muhammad over a period 23 years.
Ramadan	The ninth month of the Islamic calendar in which all healthy adults are required to abstain from all food and drink from dawn to sunset.
Salah	The obligatory five daily prayers.
Surah	A chapter of the Qur'an. The 114 surahs – are chapters of varying length.
Tarbiyyah	Holistic upbringing and education of a child.
Tawhid	Belief in the Oneness or omnipresence of God.
Umrah	The optional, lesser pilgrimage to Makkah, lasting a few hours (unlike the Hajj, which lasts for 6–7 days).
Zakat	Literal meaning is 'to purify, to grow'. It is an obligatory charity contribution, which should equal the sum of 2.5 per cent of a person's total wealth over one year, given to those in need.

| FSM | Free school meals are a statutory benefit for children to receive a daily free meal at school if their parents receive an income-based benefit from the UK government. See www.freeschoolmeals.com for more information. |

References

Abbas, T. (2007) 'Muslim Minorities in Britain: Integration, multiculturalism and radicalism in the post-7/7 Period'. *Intercultural Studies*, 28 (3), 287–300.

Abbey, S. and O'Reilly, A. (eds) (1998) *Redefining Motherhood: Changing identities and patterns*. Toronto: Second Story Press.

Afshar, H. (2008) 'Can I see your hair? Choice, agency and attitudes: The dilemma of faith and feminism for Muslim women who cover'. *Ethnic and Racial Studies*, 31 (2), 411–27.

Anthias, F. (2002) 'Where do I belong?: Narrating collective identity and translocational positionality'. *Ethnicities*, 2, 491.

— (2011) 'Intersections and translocations: New paradigms for thinking about cultural diversity and social identities'. *European Educational Research Journal*, 10 (2), 204–17.

Apple, M. (2005) 'Between neo and post: Critique and transformation in critical educational studies'. In Carl, E. and Grant, M. (eds) *Multicultural Research: Race, class, gender and sexual orientation*. London: Routledge.

Archer, L. (2010) '"We raised it with the Head": The educational practices of minority ethnic, middle-class families'. *British Journal of Sociology of Education*, 31 (4), 449–69.

Bagele, C. (2006) 'Sex education: Subjugated discourses and adolescent voices'. In Skelton, C., Francis, B. and Smulyan, L. (eds) *The SAGE Handbook of Gender and Education*. London: SAGE.

Bagley, C. and Beach, D. (2015) 'The marginalisation of social justice as a form of knowledge in teacher education in England'. *Policy Futures in Education*, 13 (4), 424–38.

Baker, P., Gabrielatos, C. and McEnery, A. (2012) *Representations of Islam in the British Press 1998–2009*. Lancaster: ERSC Centre for Corpus Approaches to Social Sciences, Lancaster University. Online. http://cass.lancs.ac.uk/wp-content/uploads/2013/12/CASS-Islam-final.pdf (accessed 2 November 2016).

Ball, S. and Vincent, C. (1998) '"I heard it on the grapevine": "Hot" knowledge and school choice'. *British Journal of Sociology of Education*, 19 (3), 377–400.

Ball, S. (2003) *Class Strategies and the Education Market: The middle classes and social advantage*. London: RoutledgeFalmer.

— (2008) *The Education Debate*. Bristol: Polity.

— (2013) *Education, Justice and Democracy: The struggle over ignorance and opportunity*. London: Centre for Labour and Social Studies.

Basit, T. (2012) 'My parents have stressed that since I was a kid: Young minority ethnic British citizens and the phenomenon of aspirational capital'. *Education, Citizenship and Social Justice*, 7 (2) 129–43.

bell hooks (1989) *Talking Back*. Boston, MA: South End Press.

Bhatti, G. (2011) 'Outsiders or insiders? Identity, educational success and Muslim young men in England'. *Ethnography and Education*, 6 (1), 81–96.

Bhimji, F. (2012) *British Asian Muslim Women: Multiple spatialities and cosmopolitanism*. Basingstoke: Palgrave Macmillan.

Birks, M. and Mills, J (2015) *Grounded Theory: A Practical Guide*. London: Sage.

Blaikie, N. (2000) *Designing Social Research: The logic of anticipation*. Oxford: Polity Press.

Bolleton, B. and Richardson, R. (2015) *The Great British Values Disaster: Education, security and vitriolic hate*. London: The Institute of Race Relations. Online. www.irr.org.uk/news/the-great-british-values-disaster-education-security-and-vitriolic-hate/ (accessed 2 November 2016).

Bourdieu, P. and Passeron, J.C. (1997) *Reproduction in Education, Society and Culture*. London: SAGE Publications.

Bowden, G. (2016) 'Muslim women speak out on language requirements, integration and extremism'. *The Huffington Post*, 9 March. Online. www.huffingtonpost.co.uk/2016/03/09/muslim-women-english-language-integration-extremism_n_9415904.html (accessed 2 November 2016).

Burgess, S. (2009) *What Parents Want: School preferences and school choice*. Bristol: Centre for Market and Public Organisation, University of Bristol.

Busby, E. (2016) 'School anti-terror referrals surge amid "climate of fear"'. *Times Educational Supplement*. Online. www.tes.com/news/school-news/breaking-news/exclusive-school-anti-terror-referrals-surge-amid-climate-fear (accessed 23 September 2016).

Cantle, T. (2001) *Community Cohesion: Report of the Independent Review Team*. London: Home Office.

Centre for Social Justice (2011) *Mental Health: Poverty, ethnicity and family breakdown*. London: The Centre for Social Justice.

Chanda-Gool, S. (2006) *South Asian Communities: Catalysts for educational change*. Stoke-on-Trent: Trentham Books Ltd.

Change Institute (2009) *Understanding Muslim Ethnic Communities: The Somali Muslim community in England*. London: Communities and Local Government.

Charmaz, K. (2008) 'Shifting the grounds: Constructivist grounded theory method'. In Morse, J. (ed.) *Developing Grounded Theory: The second generation*. Walnut Creek, CA: Left Coast Press.

Chilisa, B. (2006) 'Sex education: Subjugated discourses and adolescents' voices'. In Skelton, C., Francis, B. and Smulyan, L. (eds) *The SAGE Handbook of Gender and Education*. London: SAGE.

Choudhury, T. and Fenwick, H. (2011) *The Impact of Counter-Terrorism Measures on Muslim Communities*. Project Report 72. Manchester: Equality and Human Rights Commission.

Cole, M. (2015) *Towards the Compassionate School: From golden rule to golden thread*. London: Trentham Books at UCL IOE Press.

Crozier, G. (1999) 'Parental involvement: Who wants it?'. *International Studies in Sociology of Education*, 9 (3), 219–38.

Crozier, G. and Davies, J. (2007) 'Hard to reach parents or hard to reach schools? A discussion of home–school relations, with particular reference to Bangladeshi and Pakistani parents'. *British Educational Research Journal*, 33 (3), 295–313.

Crozier, G. and Reay, D. (eds) (2005) *Activating Participation: Parents and teachers working towards partnership*. Stoke-on-Trent: Trentham Books Ltd.

David, M. (1999) 'Home, work, families and children: New Labour, new directions, new dilemma'. *International Studies in Sociology of Education*, 9 (2), 111–32.

References

Department for Communities and Local Government (2016) '"Passive tolerance" of separate communities must end, says PM'. Online. www.gov.uk/government/news/passive-tolerance-of-separate-communities-must-end-says-pm (accessed 23 September 2016).

Department for Education (DfE) (2013a) *The National Curriculum.* Online. https://www.gov.uk/national-curriculum/other-compulsory-subjects (accessed 23 September 2016).

— (2013b) 'Guidance about teaching personal, social, health and economic education (PSHE) in England'. Online. https://www.gov.uk/government/publications/personal-social-health-and-economic-education-pshe (accessed 2 November 2016).

— (2014) *Governors' Handbook: For governors in maintained schools, academies and free schools.* Online. https://www.gov.uk/government/uploads/system/uploads/attachment_data/file/270398/Governors-Handbook-January-2014.pdf (accessed 2 November 2016).

Department for Education and Skills (DfES) (2007) *Every Parent Matters.* London: DfES.

Edwards, R. and Gillies, V. (2011) 'Clients or consumers, commonplace or pioneers? Navigating the contemporary class politics of family, parenting skills and education'. *Ethics and Education,* 6 (2), 141–54.

Elliot, J. (2005) *Using Narrative in Social Research: Quantitative and qualitative approaches.* London: SAGE.

Ellis, A. (2003) *Barriers to Participation for under-Represented Groups in School Governance.* London: Institute for Volunteering Research.

— (2009) *Barriers to Participation for Under Represented Groups in School Governance.* London: Institute for Volunteering Research.

Equality Act 2010. Online. www.legislation.gov.uk/ukpga/2010/15/pdfs/ukpga_20100015_en.pdf (accessed 23 September 2016).

Exley, S. (2011) 'School choice: Parental freedom to choose and educational equality'. In Park, A., Clery, E., Curtice, J., Phillips, M. and Utting, D. (eds) *British Social Attitudes 2011–2012.* London: SAGE.

Faith Associates (2016) *Madrassah Management Training Rolled out at Locations throughout England.* London: Faith Associates. Online. www.faithassociates.co.uk/services/madrassah-management-training/ (accessed 2 November 2016).

Gaine, C. and Lamley, K. (2003) *Racism and the Dorset Idyll: A report of the experiences of Black and minority ethnic people in Bournemouth.* Bournemouth: Dorset Race Equality Council.

Gewirtz, S., Ball, S. and Bowe, R. (1995) *Markets, Choice and Equity in Education.* Buckingham: Open University Press.

Gillies, V. (2006) 'Working class mothers and school life: Exploring the role of emotional capital'. *Gender and Education,* 18 (3), 281–93.

— (2007) *Marginalised Mothers: Exploring working class experiences of parenting.* Abingdon: Routledge.

Gilroy, P. (1997) 'Diaspora and the detours of identity'. In Woodward, K. (ed.) *Identity and Difference.* Milton Keynes: Open University Press.

Glaser, B.G. and Strauss, A.L. (1967) *The Discovery of Grounded Theory: Strategies for qualitative research.* New York: Aldine.

Goodall, H.L. Jr. (2008) *Writing Qualitative Inquiry: Self, stories and academic life*. Walnut Creek, CA: Left Coast Press.

Goodall, J. (2015a) 'School inspections leaving parents at the periphery. *The Conversation*. Online. https://theconversation.com/are-ofsteds-school-inspections-leaving-parents-at-the-periphery-49397 (accessed 2 November 2016).

— (2015b) 'We can't keep holding schools responsible for the education of our children – parents matter too'. *The Conversation*. Online. https://theconversation.com/we-cant-keep-holding-schools-responsible-for-the-education-of-our-children-parents-matter-too-43159 (accessed 2 November 2016).

Goodall, J. and Vorhaus, J. (2011) *Review of Best Practice in Parental Engagement*. London: Department for Education.

Greater London Authority (GLA) (2006) 'The Search for Common-ground: Muslims, non-Muslims and the mediational press'. London: GLA. Online. www.insted.co.uk/executive-summary.pdf (accessed 2 November 2016).

Griffiths, M. (1998) *Educational Research for Social Justice: Getting off the fence – Doing qualitative research in educational settings*. Buckingham: Open University Press.

Haleem M.A. (2010) *Understanding the Qur'an: Themes and Styles*. London: I.B Tauris.

Halsey, A.H. and Young, M. (1997) 'The family and social justice'. In Halsey, A.H., Lauder, H., Brown, P. and Wells, A.S. (eds) *Education: Culture, economy, society*. Oxford: Oxford University Press.

Harris, H. (2004) *The Somali Community in the UK: What we know and how we know it*. London: Information Centre about Asylum and Refugees (ICAR), King's College London.

Haw, K. (1998) *Educating Muslim Girls: Shifting discourses, feminist educational thinking*. Buckingham: Open University Press.

Hays, S. (1996) *The Cultural Contradictions of Motherhood*. New Haven, CT: Yale University Press.

Hollway, W. (2015) *Knowing Mothers: Researching maternal identity change*. London: Palgrave Macmillan.

Home Office (2011) *Contest: The United Kingdom's strategy for countering terrorism*. London: Home Office. Online. https://www.gov.uk/government/uploads/system/uploads/attachment_data/file/97995/strategy-contest.pdf (accessed 23 September 2016).

Hood, S. and Ouston, J. (2000) 'Home-school agreements: A true partnership?' Paper presented at the British Educational Research Association Conference held at Cardiff University.

House of Commons Education Committee (2015) *Life Lessons: PSHE and SRE in schools*. London: Stationery Office.

Hughes, L. (2016) 'More Muslim women should learn English to help tackle extremism'. *The Telegraph*, 17 January. Online. www.telegraph.co.uk/news/uknews/terrorism-in-the-uk/12104556/David-Cameron-More-Muslim-women-should-learn-English-to-help-tackle-extremism.html (accessed 2 November 2016).

References

Hussain, H. (2013) *Health in the Somali Community (Hounslow)*. London: Evelyn Oldfield Unit.

Ijaz, A. and Abbas, T. (2010) 'The impact of intergenerational change on the attitudes of working class South Asian Muslim parents on the education of their daughters'. *Gender and Education*, 22, 313–26.

Institute for Race Relations (2015) *The Great British Values Disaster*. London: IRR. Online. www.irr.org.uk/news/the-great-british-values-disaster-education-security-and-vitriolic-hate/ (2 November 2016).

Ipgrave, J. (2010) 'Including the religious viewpoints and experiences of Muslim students in an environment that is both plural and secular'. *International Migration and Integration*, 11 (5), 22.

Jackson, A.Y. and Mazzei, L.A. (eds) (2009) *Voice in Qualitative Inquiry: Challenging conventional, interpretive, and critical conceptions in qualitative research*. London: Routledge.

Khan, K. (2009) *Preventing Violent Extremism (PVE) and Prevent: A response from the Muslim community*. London: An-Nisa.

Khan, O., Ahmet, A. and Victor, C. (2014) *Poverty and Ethnicity: Balancing caring and earning for British Caribbean, Pakistani and Somali people*. York: Joseph Rowntree Foundation.

Khattab, N. and Johnston, R. (2014) 'Ethno-religious identities and persisting penalties in the UK labour market'. *The Social Science Journal*, 52 (4), 490–502.

Laureau, A. (1997) 'Social class differences in family–school relationships: The importance of cultural capital'. In Halsey, A.H., Lauder, H., Brown, P. and Wells, A.S. (eds) *Education Culture, Economy, and Society*. Oxford: OUP.

Lazarre, J. (1976) *The Mother Knot*. London: Virago Press.

Mason, S. (2010) 'Braving it out! An illuminative evaluation of the provision of sex and relationship education in two primary schools in England'. *Sex Education*, 10 (2), 157–69.

Mazzei, L. (2008) 'An impossibly full voice'. In Jackson, A. and Mazzei, L. (eds) *Voice in Qualitative Inquiry: Challenging conventional, interpretive and critical conceptions in qualitative research*. London: Routledge.

Mercer, J. (2007) 'The challenges of insider research in educational institutions: Wielding a double-edged sword and resolving delicate dilemmas'. *Oxford Review of Education*, 33 (1), 1–17.

Mirza, H. (1992) *Young, Female and Black*. London: Routledge.

— (1998) 'Same voices, same lives? Revisiting Black feminist standpoint epistemology'. In Connolly, P. and Troyna, B. (eds) *Researching 'Race' in Educational Settings: Politics, theory and practice*. Buckingham: Open University Press.

Mirza, H. and Meetoo, V. (2013) 'Gendered surveillance and the social construction of young Muslim women in schools'. In Bhopa, K. and Maylor, U. (eds) *(In)equalities: Race, Class and Gender*. London: Routledge.

Modood, T. (2005) *Multicultural Politics: Racism, ethnicity, and Muslims in Britain*. Minnesota: University of Minnesota Press.

— (2007) *Multiculturalism*. Cambridge: Polity.

Morgan, D. (1998) *Planning Focus Groups*. Thousand Oaks, CA: SAGE.

Oakley, A. (1981) 'Interviewing women: A contradiction in terms'. In Roberts, H. (1997) *Doing Feminist Research*. London: Routledge and Kegan Paul.

O'Brien, L. and Sawandar, B. (2006) *Writing the Motherline: Mothers, daughters and education*. Lanham, MA: University Press of America.

Office for National Statistics (ONS) (2011) *Language in English and Wales*. London: ONS. Online. www.ons.gov.uk/peoplepopulationandcommunity/culturalidentity/language/articles/languageinenglandandwales/2013-03-04 (accessed 2 November 2016).

— (2013) *Full story: What does the Census tell us about religion in 2011?* London: ONS. Online. http://webarchive.nationalarchives.gov.uk/20160105160709/http://www.ons.gov.uk/ons/dcp171776_310454.pdf (accessed 23 September 2016).

Office for Standards in Education (Ofsted) (2012) *Outstanding Sex and Relationship Education in a Catholic Context: The John Henry Newman Catholic School*. London: HMSO.

— (2015) *School Inspection Handbook*. Online. www.ofsted.gov.uk/resources/120101 (accessed 2 November 2016).

Open Society (2014) *Somalis in London*. Online. www.opensocietyfoundations.org/sites/default/files/somalis-london-20141010.pdf (accessed 2 November 2016).

Ouston, J. and Hood, S. (2000) 'Home-school agreements: A true partnership?' Paper presented at the British Educational Research Association's Conference at Cardiff University, 7–10 September 2000.

Pezella, A.E., Pettigrew, J. and Miller-Day, M. (2012) 'Researching the researcher-as-instrument: An exercise in interviewer self-reflexivity'. *Qualitative Research*, 12 (2), 165–85.

Phillips, D. (2009) 'Creating home spaces: Young British Muslim women's identity and conceptualisations of home'. In Hopkins, P. and Gale, R. (eds) *Muslims in Britain: Race, place and identities*. Edinburgh: Edinburgh University Press.

Piela, A. (2011) 'Piety as a concept underpinning Muslim women's online discussions of marriage and professional career'. *Contemporary Islam*, 5 (3), 249–65.

— (2012) *Muslim Women Online: Faith and identity in the virtual space*. London: Routledge.

Pre-school Learning Alliance (2007) *Information Pack for Family Learning: A resource for early years practitioners*. London: Pre-School Learning Alliance

Raith, L., Jones, J. and Porter, M. (2015) *Mothers at the Margins: Stories of challenge, resistance and love*. Newcastle upon Tyne: Cambridge Scholars.

Reay, D. (1998) 'Cultural reproduction: Mothers' involvement in their children's primary schooling'. In Grenfell, M. and James, D. (eds) *Bourdieu and Education: Acts of practical theory*. London: Falmer.

— (2000) 'A useful extension of Bourdieu's conceptual framework? Emotional capital as a way of understanding mothers' involvement in their children's education'. *The Sociological Review*, 48 (4), 568–85.

— (2005) *Class Work: Mothers' Involvement in their Children's Primary Schooling*. London: Taylor and Francis e-Library.

Ribbens, J. (1994) *Mothers and their Children: A feminist sociology of childrearing*. London: SAGE.

References

Ribbens McCarthy, J. and Kirkpatrick, S. (2005) 'Negotiating public and private: Maternal mediations of home-school boundaries'. In Crozier, G. and Reay, D. (eds) *Activating Participation: Parents and teachers working towards partnership*. London: Trentham Books Ltd.

Rich, A. (1995 [1976]) *Of Woman Born: Motherhood as experience and institution*. New York: W.W. Norton.

Rollock, N. (2009) *School Governors and Race Equality in 21st Century Schools*. Runnymede Briefing Paper. London: Runnymede Trust. Online. www.runnymedetrust.org/uploads/publications/pdfs/SchoolGovernors-2009.pdf (accessed 2 November 2016).

Rubin, H.J. and Rubin, I.S. (2012) *Qualitative Interviewing: The art of hearing data*. Thousand Oaks, CA: SAGE.

Ruddick, S. (1989) *Maternal Thinking: Towards a politics of peace*. New York: The Women's Press.

Saeed, A. (2007) 'British Muslims are portrayed as an "alien other" within the media'. *Sociology Compass*, 1 (2), 443–62.

Salmons, J. (2015) *Doing Qualitative Research Online*. London: SAGE.

Schliefer, A. (1996) *Motherhood in Islam*. Kentucky: The Islamic Texts Society.

— (1997) *Mary the Blessed Virgin of Islam*. Louisville: Fons Vitae.

Seale, C. (1999) *The Quality of Qualitative Research*. London: SAGE.

Secretaries of State for Education and Wales (1992) *Choice and Diversity in Schools: A new framework for schools* (White Paper). London: HMSO.

Shain, F. (2003) *The Schooling and Identity of Asian Girls*. Stoke-on-Trent: Trentham Books Ltd.

— (2012) 'Getting on rather than getting by: Ethnicity, class and 'success against the odds'. *British Journal of Sociology of Education*, 33 (1), 153–63.

Simon, S. and Bryan S.T. (eds) (2011) *The Legacy of Pierre Bourdieu Critical Essays*. London: Anthem Press.

Sporton, D. and Valentine, G. (2007) *Identities on the Move: The integration experiences of Somali refugee and asylum seeker young people*. Sheffield and Leeds: University of Leeds and University of Sheffield.

Scourfield, J., Gilliat-Ray, S., Khan, A. and Otri, S. (2013) *Muslim Childhood: Religious nurture in a European context*. Oxford: Oxford University Press.

Sundas, A. (2015) *British Muslims in Numbers: A demographic, socio-economic and health profile of Muslims in Britain drawing on the 2011 Census*. London: Muslim Council of Britain.

The Independent (2014) 'Muslim mothers should be trained in computing "to help to spot radicalisation"', 6 January. Online. www.independent.co.uk/news/uk/home-news/muslim-mothers-should-be-trained-in-computing-to-help-to-spot-radicalisation-9040289.html (accessed 2 November 2016).

Veazey, L.W. (2015) 'Motherhood and intersectionality'. Paper given at the *TASA Gender and Families Symposium*, 30–31 October 2015.

Vincent, C. (1996) 'Parent empowerment? Collective action and inaction in education'. *Oxford Review of Education*, 22 (4), 465–82.

— (2000) *Including Parents? Education, Citizenship and Parental Agency*. Milton Keynes: Open University Press.

Vincent, C., Ball, S. and Braun, A. (2010) 'Between the estate and the state: Struggling to be a "good" mother'. *British Journal of Sociology of Education*, 31 (2), 123–38.

Vincent, C. and Martin, J. (2002) 'Class, culture and agency: Researching parental voice'. *Discourse*, 23 (1), 109–28.

Webber, F. (2016) *Prevent and the Children's Right's Convention*. London: Institute of Race Relations.

Wilkins, C. (2014) 'Inspecting the inspectors: Race equality and quality in initial teacher education'. *Race, Ethnicity and Education*, 17 (3), 445–70.

Williams, N. (2015) 'The skin I'm in: From the margins to the centre'. In Raith, L., Jones, J. and Porter, M. (eds) *Mothers at the Margin: Stories of challenge, resistance and love*. Newcastle upon Tyne: Cambridge Scholars.

Yosso, T. (2005) 'Whose culture has capital? A critical race theory discussion of community cultural wealth'. *Race, Ethnicity and Education*, 8 (1), 69–91.

Index